THE BALANCE OF PAYMENTS ANALYSIS
OF DEVELOPING ECONOMIES

T0372542

The Balance of Payments Analysis of Developing Economies

Evidence from Nigeria and Ghana

OLUMUYIWA SAMSON ADEDEJI
International Monetary Fund, USA

JAGDISH HANDA
McGill University, Canada

and

ALEXANDER BILSON DARKU
Concordia University, Canada

Routledge
Taylor & Francis Group

LONDON AND NEW YORK

First published 2005 by Ashgate Publishing

Reissued 2018 by Routledge
2 Park Square, Milton Park, Abingdon, Oxon OX14 4RN
605 Third Avenue, New York, NY 10017

First issued in paperback 2021

Routledge is an imprint of the Taylor & Francis Group, an informa business

A Library of Congress record exists under LC control number: 2005022766

Notice:
Product or corporate names may be trademarks or registered trademarks, and are used only for identification and explanation without intent to infringe.

Publisher's Note
The publisher has gone to great lengths to ensure the quality of this reprint but points out that some imperfections in the original copies may be apparent.

Disclaimer
The publisher has made every effort to trace copyright holders and welcomes correspondence from those they have been unable to contact.

ISBN 13: 978-0-815-39748-9 (hbk)
ISBN 13: 978-1-351-14764-4 (ebk)
ISBN 13: 978-1-138-35739-6 (pbk)

DOI: 10.4324/9781351147644

Contents

Preface

West African economies have been characterized in recent decades by recurrent current account deficits and continual increases in external debt. This pattern of recurring current account deficits coupled with secular growth of the external debt is common to developing countries generally, and is quite pronounced in the Sub-Saharan context. Another common feature is the seeming excessiveness and unsustainability of the external imbalances. These features, widely shared among developing economies, provided the motivation for the theoretical and empirical researches carried out in this book.

This book presents the theoretical and econometric analysis of the current account of the balance of payments of Nigeria and Ghana. These two countries are the two English-speaking ones in West African and share many common economic characteristics and strands of political history.

The book has two major objectives. The first is to present the theoretical modifications of the standard version of the present value model of the current account (PVMCA) to reflect the major features of the English-speaking West African economies. For the empirical part of this, the book uses econometric analysis to determine if the resulting theoretical models are valid for the analysis of the current account balances of these economies. The second objective is to examine the excessiveness and sustainability of their current account deficits.

To achieve these objectives, the book presents an intertemporal model of current account determination based upon the permanent income hypothesis of private consumption. This hypothesis is used as a starting point to derive the present value model of the current account (PVMCA). The PVMCA is essentially an intertemporal approach that treats the current account of the balance of payments as a buffer for smoothing consumption in the face of shocks affecting output, investment and government expenditures. The standard version of this model assumes that the home country and the rest of the world produce goods that are identical (so that there is no direct role for the terms of trade), a constant real interest rate (so that there is no role for consumption tilting effects), zero transport costs, and all goods are tradable across countries (so that it excludes nontradable goods and a role for movements in the real exchange rate). However, two findings of the empirical studies using the standard PVMCA are of particular concern. First, many studies have found the actual current account to be more volatile than the optimal one. Second, the statistical restrictions implied by these models have been rejected for a number of countries. These assumptions have limited the empirical success of the standard PVMCA in the literature.

A more realistic analysis needs to relax several of these assumptions. In particular, it is necessary to eliminate the assumption of a single good and to allow for a distinction between tradable and nontradable goods. In doing so, this book extends the standard PVMCA to incorporate, at the theoretical level, changes in the interest rate, exchange rate and terms of trade. A change in the terms of trade impacts on the current account through a number of channels. Among these is that an unanticipated deterioration in the terms of trade reduces current income below its permanent level, which leads to a deterioration in the current account balance. In addition, the deterioration in the terms of trade also induces domestic economic agents to increase their relative demand for nontradables, leading to an increase in the relative price of non-tradable goods, with consequent negative impact on the current account balance. Further, the increase in the current prices of importables relative to their future prices induces agents to tilt consumption towards the future, thereby reducing current consumption. This book uses the consumption-based interest rate to capture the likely effects of changes in both the terms of trade and exchange rates. The modified PVMCA incorporating the consumption-based interest rate is further extended to accommodate asymmetry in the access to the international financial markets.

This book presents the empirical estimation of the several variants of the PVMCA developed in this book. The econometric results for Nigeria and Ghana show that the intertemporal model that includes changes in the interest rate, exchange rate and terms of trade outperforms those PVMCA models that exclude these variables. Our empirical findings indicate that the intertemporal approach constitutes an appropriate approach for examining the current account. However, the actual current account balances are more volatile than the optimal ones, indicating that speculative factors are a significant driving force behind capital flows.

For comparison with our findings from the PVMCA approach, this book also performs the empirical analyses of current account determination using the traditional elasticity, absorption and monetary approaches.

In addition, this book presents the theoretical and empirical analysis for assessing the excessiveness of the actual current account balances relative to the optimal ones. Such an assessment has to be based on a theoretical analysis that can determine the optimal current account balance, which can then be compared with the actual one. This book uses the PVMCA to derive the optimal current account balances and then to assess the excessiveness of the actual current account balances. This assessment was based on a wide range of economic indicators. Our findings on this question indicate that:

- The current account deficits associated with exchange rate appreciations and fiscal deficits appear not to be sustainable.
- The period following oil price shocks showed relatively greater response of the current account balances to expected changes in net output.
- The optimal current account deficits under asymmetric access to the international financial market were greater than those with unrestricted access.

- Current account deficits accompanied by macroeconomic instability and structural weaknesses generate external crises.

Our findings for Nigeria and Ghana are very similar. This should not come as a surprise since they share many common economic – including the stage of economic development – and political characteristics, except to the extent of one being an oil-exporting country and the other an oil-importing one.

In terms of our policy recommendations, Nigeria and Ghana, given their extreme vulnerability to shocks, are likely to be better off maintaining flexible exchange rate regimes. Further, our review of Nigeria's and Ghana's macroeconomics indicators over the past four decades shows the overriding importance of supportive macroeconomic discipline, including that on fiscal deficits, if unsustainable current account deficits and a large premium is to be avoided in a parallel exchange market in the case of a fixed regime or perpetual depreciation in the case of a floating regime.

In terms of contributions to the general literature on the current account determination of developing countries, this book derives several variants of the intertemporal approach to the current account especially applicable to them. In particular, this book represents the first attempt at incorporating into the PVMCA two features relevant to developing countries: changes in the terms of trade and asymmetry in access to the international financial markets. It also illustrates the incorporation into the PVMCA of changes in the interest and exchange rates, the oil price shocks and policy shifts. Further, this book presents the analysis and empirical procedures for assessing the excessiveness and sustainability of the current account deficits. These are also applicable to other developing countries.

This book draws heavily on Adedeji (2001a, 20001b, 2002), Adedeji and Handa (2005a, 2005b) and Darku and Handa (2005).

The views expressed in the book are those of the authors and should not be interpreted as those of the IMF or of the other institutions with which the authors are associated.

We are grateful to numerous individuals for their suggestions and comments. These include, among others, Franque Grimard at McGill University, and Stanley Black, Ulrich Bartsch, Eric Clifton, Oeyvind Maehle, Saleh Nsouli and John Thornton, at the IMF, as well as several referees of this book and our papers on which we have drawn. We also owe thanks to a number of persons who provided valuable assistance in many other ways. These include Omar Hayat and Abdul Rahman for assistance in formatting the final copy.

Chapter 1

Introduction

Nigeria and Ghana are the two largest English-speaking economies in West Africa and share many economic characteristics, as well as several aspects of economic and political history. Since Nigeria's independence in 1960 and Ghana's in 1957, both countries have been characterized by recurrent current account deficits and continual increases in external debt. The ratio of the external debt to GDP for Nigeria was 10 percent in 1970, reached 110 percent in 1986 and stood at approximately 71 percent in 1997. The corresponding figures for Ghana were 25 percent, 48 percent and 102 percent. The recurring current account deficits coupled with the evolution of the external debt call for research into the determinants, excessiveness and sustainability of the external imbalances of these two countries. This examination requires a formal model that gives the optimal current account balance, which can then be compared with the actual one. This book uses the present value model of the current account (PVMCA) to derive the optimal current account balances for Nigeria and Ghana and then to assess the excessiveness of the actual current account balances during the period 1960-97.

As against the traditional elasticities, absorption and monetary approaches to the current account, the PVMCA is an intertemporal approach that treats the current account as a buffer for smoothing domestic consumption in the face of shocks affecting output, investment and government expenditures. This approach to current account determination has its origin in Campbell and Shiller's (1987) seminal work on the relationship between current saving and the expected change in labour income. In current account modelling, saving or dissaving during the period determines the current account balance during a period, and the expected change in the net output (GDP minus investment minus government expenditure) acts as the expected change in labour income.

The standard (designated in this book as the 'benchmark') version of the PVMCA assumes that: the home country and the rest of the world produce goods that are physically identical (so that there is no direct role for the terms of trade), a constant real interest rate (so that there is no role for consumption tilting effects), zero transport costs, and all goods are tradable across countries (so that it excludes nontradable goods and a role for movements in the real exchange rate). These assumptions have limited the empirical success of the benchmark PVMCA. A more realistic analysis needs to relax several of these assumptions. In particular, it is necessary to eliminate the assumption of a single good and allow for a distinction between tradable and nontradable goods.

Further, two findings of the benchmark PVMCA are of particular concern. First, many studies have found the actual current account to be more volatile than the optimal.[1] Second, the statistical restrictions implied by these models have been rejected for a considerable number of countries.

This book modifies the PVMCA to incorporate at the theoretical level changes in the interest rate, exchange rates and terms of trade. Changes in the terms of trade are considered important for both Nigeria and Ghana. A change in the terms of trade impacts on the current account through a number of channels. First, an unanticipated deterioration in the terms of trade, with a constant consumption level, reduces current income below its permanent level, which tends to produce deterioration in the current account balance. Second, the increase in the current prices of importables relative to their future prices induces agents to tilt consumption towards the future, thereby reducing current consumption. Third, the deterioration in the terms of trade affects the current account through changes in the exchange rate: the deterioration in the terms of trade induces domestic economic agents to increase their relative demand for nontradables, leading to an increase in the relative price of nontradables (exchange rate appreciation), with consequent negative impact on the current account balance. This book uses a consumption-based interest rate to capture the expected changes in both terms of trade and exchange rates. The model incorporating the consumption-based interest rate is then extended to accommodate possible restrictions on access to the international financial markets.

Our empirical findings for both Nigeria and Ghana indicate that the intertemporal approach constitutes an appropriate approach for examining the current account. This assessment is based on the following findings:

- The optimal and actual current account balances were stationary variables, as predicted by the PVMCA.
- The statistical restrictions implied by the PVMCA were not rejected when changes in the interest rate, exchange rate and terms of trade were considered.
- The optimal current account balances derived from the PVMCA were able to capture the evolution of the actual current account balance.
- For Nigeria, the introduction of the Structural Adjustment Program in 1986 did not alter the relationship between the change in net output and the current account, though the post-oil-price-shock periods were marked by a relatively greater response of the current account to expected changes in net output.

For both Nigeria and Ghana, the actual current account proved to be more volatile than the optimal one, indicating that speculative factors were a major

---

[1]   Given the available mixed results, Otto (1992), Milbourne and Otto (1992), Sheffrin and Woo (1990), among others, speculated that, for a small open economy, the current account might be more affected by temporary changes in resource prices.

driving force behind capital flows. Our empirical analysis also showed that the optimal current account deficits in the presence of restricted access to the international financial market were greater than those with unrestricted access. This suggests that, in the face of unexpected shocks, the economic agents in both countries were not able to use the international financial markets to the extent that they would have desired. In addition, the hypothesis of asymmetric access to the international financial market helps to explain the excessiveness in the current account balances for the period 1990-1997 for the Ghanaian economy and the period prior to 1986 for the Nigerian economy.

To incorporate some of the distinct features of the Nigerian experience, we took account of the oil price shock of 1973 and the introduction of the Structural Adjustment Program in 1986. For comparison with our estimates from the PVMCA approach, this book also performs for Nigeria the empirical analysis of the current account determination using the more traditional elasticity, absorption and monetary approaches. The use of various macroeconomic indicators to assess the sustainability of the Nigerian current account deficits shows that the assessment of the sustainability of external imbalances must be based on a wide range of relevant macroeconomic indicators. Current account deficits associated with exchange rate appreciation and fiscal deficits appear not to be sustainable. When associated with low savings, a high concentration of exports in a particular commodity, lower economic growth, growing external debt, high debt servicing, inadequate foreign exchange reserves and political instability, our findings indicate that current account deficits can degenerate into an external crisis. For Nigeria, in the period preceding 1986, especially 1981-83, the current account balances were persistently excessive. The strict trade and exchange policies followed during 1984-85 did curb this trend. However, the unsustainability of the policies adopted was reflected in a dramatic widening of the gap between the optimal and actual current account balance in 1986.

Theoretical and empirical contributions

This book covers a longer data span than previous econometric studies of Nigeria's and Ghana's current account determination.

For the Nigerian and Ghanaian economies, this book is the first attempt at estimating a PVMCA that includes changes in interest rate, exchange rate and at the same time accommodates the oil price shocks of 1973.

This book assesses the sustainability of the current account balance by examining the macroeconomic variables that reflect the structure of the Nigerian and Ghanaian economies, the policy stance of the government and political economy factors. In doing this, this book is the first in-depth analysis for sub-Saharan African countries based on the present value model of the current account and using the concepts of the excessiveness and sustainability of current account deficits.

For developing economies generally, this book represents the first attempt at incorporating the terms of trade in an intertemporal model of the current account, as well as accommodating possible asymmetry in access to the international financial market.

Our results from estimating the intertemporal model of current account determination point to changes in world real interest rates, exchange rates, terms of trade and fiscal balances as important determinants of the current account. Further, they indicate the importance of considering the impact of asymmetrical capital flows in and out of the country for the current account and the balance of payments.

Chapter 2

An Overview of the Nigerian Economy and the Relevant Concepts

Introduction

This chapter has two main objectives. The first is to provide stylised facts on the Nigerian economy during the 1960-97 period covered by this book. This is important for two main reasons. First, it permits an understanding of the need to extend the basic intertemporal model of the current account to reflect changes in the exchange rate and the terms of trade. Second, a crucial issue addressed in this book is the sustainability of the Nigerian current account deficits. An understanding of the structure of the Nigerian economy is relevant to the appropriateness of the macroeconomic variables chosen to achieve this. The second objective of this chapter is to discuss relevant concepts that are explored in more detail in Chapters 4, 5 and 6.

This introduction is followed by two sections on the Nigerian economy. Section 2.1 provides information on the structure and evolution of the Nigerian economy. Section 2.2 reviews the evolution of the current account balance and other macroeconomic variables. The evolutions of these macroeconomic variables are used to characterize the occurrence of external crisis in Nigeria in 1986.[1]

2.1 An Overview of the Nigerian Economy (1960-97)

This section provides background information on the Nigerian economy during the period 1960-97. Broadly, we divide the analysis into four major periods. The first period is 1960-73. It covers the period from the year of independence up to the first oil prices shock in 1973. The second period, 1974-80, covers the period after the first oil price shock and before the emergence of serious economic recessions. The third period, 1981 to 1986, includes various austerity measures implemented by the Nigerian government prior to the adoption of the Structural Adjustment Program. The period thereafter, 1987-97, marked the post-Structural Adjustment Program era.

---

[1] Chapter 6 conducts a more extensive examination of the external position of the Nigerian economy.

The Agricultural Sector

Before the dominance of the oil sector in the 1970s, the agricultural sector was the mainstay of the Nigerian economy. As of 1960, agriculture's share of total value added was 64 percent (Data Appendix 2.II) and constituted the major source of foreign exchange earnings. The development of the oil sector reduced the importance of the agricultural sector: its share of total output declined to 34 percent by 1997. Agriculture, combined with other non-oil exports, contributed about 2 percent of the foreign exchange earnings in the 1990s.

The decline in the performance of the agricultural sector can be analysed from two perspectives. First, the decline can be perceived as a natural phenomenon, part of the developmental process. As an economy moves from one stage of development to another, the agricultural sector is expected to become less important as other sectors and GDP grow at faster rates.

Second, the decline may be the consequence of a macroeconomic policy that discriminates against the agricultural sector. Empirical evidence does seem to support this hypothesis. A number of factors have been identified as responsible for the poor agricultural performance: the failure of the commodity boards[2] to ensure consistency between set prices, domestic costs and international prices; the widening gap between the retail food prices and stagnant producer prices that engendered further transfer of resources from the agricultural sector to other sectors, especially the service sector; the use of a fixed exchange rate before 1986 that culminated in real exchange rate appreciation.

The following review of the emergence of the oil sector provides additional support to the hypothesis that the decline in the importance of the Nigerian agricultural sector may indeed have been a consequence of a macroeconomic policy that discriminated against the agricultural sector.

External Shocks and Policy Responses (1973-81)

The development of the oil industry in the early 1970s transformed Nigeria from an agrarian economy to an oil-based economy. Oil's share of total output was 12 percent in 1970, increased to 33 percent by 1974 and further increased to 39 percent by 1997 (see Data Appendix 2.II). The share of oil in total federally collected revenues increased from 26 percent in 1970 to 60 percent by 1973, reached a peak of 82 percent by 1974 and stood at 72 percent by 1997. In terms of foreign exchange earnings, the oil share of total exports was 58 percent in 1970, 83 percent by 1973, and 93 percent by 1974 and further increased to 98 percent by 1997.

The dominance of the oil sector in the 1970s and 1980s reflected significant increases in oil prices during the 1973-74 and 1979-80 periods.

---

[2] This is the board responsible for fixing the prices of agricultural export products. The idea behind this is to prevent farmers from being vulnerable to changes in agricultural export products in the international markets.

Commensurate with increases in the oil prices, both government and private consumption expenditures increased tremendously. Expanded government resources were transferred to the private sector through wage increases in the public sector.[3] The increased salary of the public sector workers resulted in the private sector worker's demands for salary increases. The increase in aggregate demand arising from the upward movement in the public sector salaries combined with increases in the cost of production associated with increases in the private sector salaries led to an increase in the general level of prices. With a fixed exchange rate regime and in the face of increases in domestic prices, the real exchange rate appreciated. This, in turn, further increased the aggregate demand in the economy and had a consequent negative impact on the current account balance.

Adverse Oil Prices Shocks and Policy Responses (1982-86)

Given the Nigerian economy's excessive dependence on petroleum export earnings, the fall in world oil prices in 1982 had a negative impact. The Nigerian economy is heavily dependent on imports of manufactured and intermediate goods, and import demand could not adjust quickly enough to declining foreign exchange receipts. To facilitate importation of these goods, the government set real exchange rates at unsustainable appreciated levels and engaged in some short and medium term borrowing, creating an increase in debt service obligations.

This policy response resulted in current account and balance of payments deficits, reduced foreign exchange reserves and an increase in external debt obligation. In response, the government put trade and exchange controls in place.

This policy of exchange controls and restrictions aimed at reducing the outflow of foreign exchange was inadequate in dealing with the current account deficit problems. The nature of exchange control administration created uncertainties among private investors that reduced incentives for private investment and encouraged corruption, rent-seeking activities, and smuggling. In addition to the impediments to trade, the nature of the exchange control mechanism introduced distortions into the economy that greatly affected its overall performance. In order to correct the level of absorption in the economy, the government introduced a number of austerity measures.

Austerity Measures and the Structural Adjustment Program

To deal with the economic problems the country was encountering, the government introduced the Economic Stabilization Act in 1982. The National Economic Emergency Act followed in 1985. Both acts focused on reducing the levels of aggregate absorption in the economy. However, these acts failed to address macroeconomic and structural problems facing the economy: the

---

[3]   The 'Udojie' award of 1975 increased salaries by over 100 percent in the government sector.

appreciated real exchange rate, the unsustainable size of the government, the over-dependence on the oil sector, and a host of other structural problems.

The government, therefore, introduced the Structural Adjustment Program (SAP) in 1986. The SAP emphasized six major policy measures: restructuring and diversifying of the productive base of the economy to reduce dependence on the oil sector and on imports; deregulation of the exchange rate; trade liberalization; deregulation of the financial sector; rationalization and privatization of public sector enterprises; and adoption of appropriate pricing policies (by eliminating subsidies), especially for petroleum products and in public enterprises. Given the policy measures introduced in 1986, it is a reasonable conclusion that 1986 was a crisis year.

Our overview of the Nigerian economy has revealed its sensitivity to external shocks, especially terms of trade shocks. The absence of a market-determined exchange rate before 1986 resulted in real exchange rate appreciation with resultant deterioration in the current account balance. It is therefore of utmost importance that any model of current account designed for Nigeria takes these variables into consideration.

In the following section, in line with the economic literature on the sustainability of the current account deficits,[4] we have chosen 1986 as the crisis year, when the Nigerian Naira massively depreciated from N1 to the US$ in 1985 to N4 to the US$ in 1986. This choice is further supported by the fact that, in 1986, Nigeria was unable to service its existing debt obligations and, recognizing the need for a policy reversal in order to reduce external imbalances, introduced economic reforms.

2.2 The Current Account Balance

In assessing the external position of a country, attention is usually paid to the current account balance. The change in the net foreign assets position of a country depends on the current account balance. As noted by McGettigan (1999), it is difficult to separate current account sustainability from external sustainability in a broader sense; consequently the terms 'current account sustainability' and 'external sustainability' are often used interchangeably. Hence, an external crisis may have its foundation in current account imbalances. In support of this proposition, Nyatepe-Coo (1993)[5] found that current account deficits assumed greater importance as the proximate source of debt build-up in Nigeria, accounting for 63 percent of the accumulated change in the external debt during the period 1981-89.

---

[4]   These studies focus exclusively on devaluation episodes. Some of them examine large and infrequent devaluations [Edwards (1989), Edwards and Montiel (1989), Edwards and Santaella (1993), Frankel and Rose (1996), Milesi-Ferretti and Razin (1996)].
[5]   This paper identified three major contributory factors to debt build-up: current account deficits, net capital outflows and capital flight.

Nigeria's current account balance has shown remarkable changes over time (Figure 2.1). The annual average of the current account balance as a ratio of GDP was about -5 percent during the period 1960-73. It ranged from -7.3 percent in 1966 to 0.5 percent in 1973.

The period 1974-80 marked a turn in the evolution of the current account balance. There were current account surpluses in 1974, 1979 and 1980, reflecting substantial increases in the crude oil prices. The current account balance showed an annual average surplus of almost 2 percent of GDP. For this period, the current account balance ranged from -7 percent in 1978 to 17 percent in 1974.

During 1981-83, the current account balance was consistently negative, standing at an annual average of 8 percent of GDP. The following two years marked current account surpluses to the magnitude of 1 percent, partly reflecting the tightening of the trade controls during the same period. The annual average of the current account deficit over the period 1981-85 was approximately 5 percent of GDP.

During the period 1986-88, the current account maintained a negative trend, with the exception of 1986. However, the following four years, 1989-92, marked current account surpluses, followed by current account deficits up to 1995. From 1996 to 1997, current account balances were positive.

The behaviour of the Nigerian current account was sensitive to developments in the world oil market, even after the introduction of the economic reforms in 1986. Among other factors, this sensitivity reflects the non-diversification of the economic base.

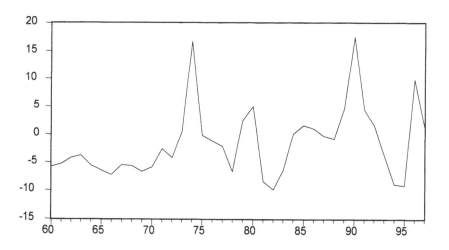

Figure 2.1 Current Account Balance (in Percent of GDP)

2.3 The Size of the External Debt

The ability of a country to sustain current account deficits is negatively affected by its stock of international liabilities. An existing large burden of external debt may reduce the willingness of the foreign economy to continue financing the current account deficit of the country concerned, as expectations mount up that the country may default on its existing external obligations. Moreover, a large debt-servicing burden can easily exhaust export revenues and prevent imports of investment goods that are needed for growth. In such a case, the debt burden can create a trap that inhibits any growth policies.

　　The external debt to GDP ratio showed an increasing trend over most of the period covered (Figure 2.2). It increased from approximately 10 percent during 1970-73 and 1974-80 to 55 percent during 1981-86 and 116 percent from 1987-1997. This increase, associated with current account deficits, especially during 1981-83, could explain the emergence of the external crisis in 1986.

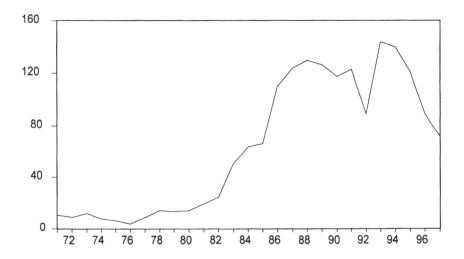

Figure 2.2   External Debt to GDP Ratio

2.4 The Real Exchange Rate[6]

When a country's real exchange rate is overvalued beyond a certain threshold level, or above an historical average, and this overvaluation is associated with

----

[6]   Data availability reduced the analysis of exchange rate movements to the period 1981-97. An increase in the real effective exchange rate in Figure 2.2 represents an appreciation and a decrease represents depreciation.

current account deficits, there is a presumption that such deficits are not sustainable.[7] Real appreciation of the currency could lead to a loss of competitiveness and increase in the consumption of imported goods, which, in turn, would result in a worsening of the current account balance. In order to remove the imbalance associated with such an appreciation, it is mandatory that the government devalue the currency of the country.

There is evidence of real exchange rate appreciation in Nigeria before the introduction of economic reforms in 1986. For the period 1981-85, the annual average appreciation of the real effective exchange rate was 14 percent (see Figure 2.3 for the evolution of the real effective exchange rate). The current account deficits over the period 1981-85 were not sustainable as they were associated with real exchange rate appreciation. In order to ensure a sustainable current account position, the government had to devalue the currency towards the end of 1986.

The introduction of economic reforms in 1986 produced a significant depreciation of the real effective exchange rate. During 1986-97, the real effective exchange rate depreciated by 12 percent. At the same time, the current account surplus was 1 percent of GDP.

2.5 The GDP Growth Rate

The higher a country's GDP growth rate, the greater the current account imbalance that it can sustain without increasing its external debt-to-GDP ratio.[8] Also, high (actual and expected) GDP growth may reflect sustained capital accumulation rates driven by expectations of high profitability. Current account deficits that are associated with higher economic performance can be considered to be sustainable. The annual average growth rate of GDP was 5 percent during the period 1960-73, pointing to the sustainability of current account deficits experienced over the same period. However, the growth rate declined to 4 percent during 1974-80 and the economy witnessed an annual average negative growth rate of 2 percent over the period 1981-85. Thus, prior to the structural adjustment reforms initiated in 1986, the economy experienced a substantial decline in the rate of growth. This declining trend in growth points to a reduction in the capacity of the country to sustain

---

[7]   It is important to distinguish between various types of real exchange rate appreciation. Real appreciation that emanates from a pegged exchange rate regime combined with inflation inertia is detrimental to the external position of the economy. On the other hand, a stabilization policy resulting in the inflow of foreign direct investment and other capital inflows can generate exchange rate appreciation. Such real appreciation may also be associated with larger current account deficits, which would be a good development reflecting increased imports of capital or intermediate goods, rather than any fundamental problem. The former form of appreciation calls for a possible devaluation in the future, while the latter may reflect an appreciation of the equilibrium exchange rate.

[8]   Section 6.7 in Chapter 6 demonstrates this postulation and uses Nigerian data to validate it.

persistent current account deficits and, consequently, the need to introduce economic reforms to remove external imbalances. Figure 2.4 shows the real growth rate of the Nigerian economy during the period 1960-97.

2.6 Fiscal Deficits

A given current account deficit may emanate from either a public savings-investment balance or a private savings-investment balance or a combination of the two. The linkage between fiscal positions and current account can be established through the equilibrium condition for the goods market that defines the current account balance as:

$$CA_t = S_t - I_t = (S_g - I_g) - (S_{pv} - I_{pv})$$ (2.1)

where CA_t is the current account balance; S_t is aggregate saving, I_t is planned investment in the economy; S_g is government saving; I_g is government investment; S_{pv} is private investment; and I_{pv} is private investment. All variables are in nominal terms.

If private sector external liabilities are not guaranteed by the government (if they are, private debts become public debt) and the private economic agents base their saving decisions on accurate forecasts of relevant economic variables, such as expected permanent income,[9] a current account deficit arising from a private saving-investment balance is considered to be more sustainable than the one arising from a public saving-investment balance.

This assumption reflects the fact that fiscal deficits may induce excessive monetary growth, generating the possibility of speculative attacks, especially under a fixed exchange rate regime. If foreign investors suspect that the government will be unwilling or unable to service its external obligation at some stage in the future, this could lead to the cessation of private capital inflows and the withdrawal of the pre-existing short-term foreign investments, culminating in an external crisis.

Government fiscal balances were in deficit in most of the years considered by this study. Over the period 1961-73, the government deficit was 2.4 percent of GDP (Figure 2.5). The stage of development of the Nigerian economy, and the market expectations that the civil war was a temporary phenomenon and that the economy had the potential for higher growth, prevented an external crisis[10] resulting from current account deficits associated with fiscal deficits.

---

[9] If not, an overly optimistic expected income can result in a current consumption level that is not sustainable.

[10] Current account deficits arising from fiscal deficits can lead to external crisis. This would be the case if the government deficits arose from low revenue tax base and unproductive investment and unsustainable consumption levels.

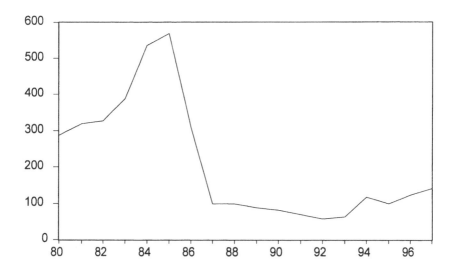

Figure 2.3　Real Effective Exchange Rate (1995 = 100)

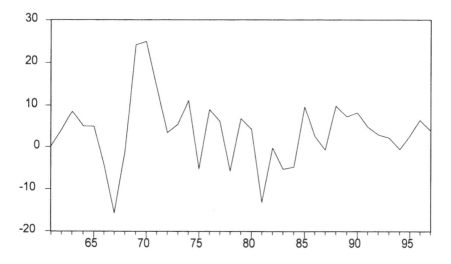

Figure 2.4　Annual GDP Growth

During the period 1974-81, the dramatic increase in the government revenues from oil exports was reflected in a reduction in fiscal deficits to 0.85 of GDP. Any deficits during such periods are more sustainable since they come from the saving-investment balance of the private sector. Thereafter, the fiscal deficit as a ratio of GDP was 7.5 percent during the 1982-86 period and 6.2 percent over the period 1987-97. As indicated earlier, current account deficits arising from government savings-investment balances could generate anticipation of higher future tax liabilities. This expectation could lead to a reduction in capital inflows and hinder the ability of the government to sustain such deficits, possibly resulting in an external crisis.

Based on this indicator, the sustainability of current account deficits is sensitive to the behaviour of the fiscal balance. Fiscal deficits (emanating from high levels of government consumption expenditure) that lead to current account deficits with resultant debt accumulation hinder the ability of the government to service its debt in the future. Rational foreign investors would tend to withdraw their capital from the country. Also, an environment of current high levels of debt discourages investment as investors anticipate that higher levels of taxes will have to be imposed in the future in order to service the current high levels of debt. Therefore, fiscal indicators constitute relevant variables for predicting the possibility of occurrence of external crisis.

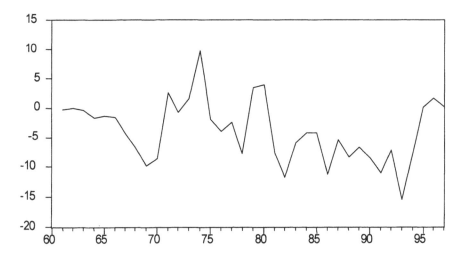

Figure 2.5   Fiscal Deficit to GDP Ratio

2.7 Adequacy of Foreign Exchange Reserves

Lower foreign exchange reserves, in a fixed exchange rate regime, indicate a reduction in the ability of a monetary authority to maintain the administratively fixed exchange rate in the event of a shock that calls for exchange rate depreciation. Economic agents, realizing the weak position of the monetary authority in defending the existing exchange rate, are prone to attack the currency, resulting in eventual currency devaluation (Krugman, 1979).

The conventional approach is to express international reserves in months of imports. However, when capital is highly mobile, this may not necessarily be the most suitable measure of reserve adequacy. An outflow of existing capital puts pressure on the exchange rate and further increases the needs to expand the foreign exchange reserves. Moreover, if reserves are low relative to short term debt servicing (irrespective of the fact that they may be sufficient to cover imports), the country may still experience an external crisis. Also, in periods of uncertainty, there are tendencies to convert liquid liabilities into foreign exchange. This puts pressure on foreign exchange reserves and increases the need to augment reserves. To capture this scenario, an alternative to the international reserves expressed in months of imports is the ratio of M2 to international reserves. This is to capture the fact that M2, which contains currency and demand plus savings deposits, is one proxy for the potential liabilities that domestic agents may wish to convert into foreign exchange in times of uncertainty.

Foreign exchange reserves in months of imports were 7 months over the period 1960-73; therefore, the financing of current account deficits was not a serious problem, since they were only about 2 percent of GDP during the same period. The foreign exchange reserves in months of imports increased to 9 months during the period 1974-80. However, they showed a downward turn, decreasing to 2 months of imports in the course of 1981-86 and remained constant at about an average of 2 months in the following period (1987-97). Figure 2.6 shows the evolution of international reserves in months of imports below.

This indicator points to the unsustainability of current account deficits over the period 1981-86 and, therefore, explains the introduction of economic reforms in 1986 that were associated with a depreciation of the exchange rate. Using the ratio of M2 to international reserves as shown in Figure 2.7 does not change this conclusion.

This chapter has reviewed the evolution of the Nigerian economy during the period 1960-97 and used the evolution of a number of macroeconomic indicators such as the current balance position, the size of external debt, the real exchange rate, the economic growth rate, fiscal deficits and adequacy of foreign exchange reserves to examine the external position of the Nigerian economy. These variables point to the unsustainability of the Nigerian current account deficits in the period preceding the external crisis of 1986.

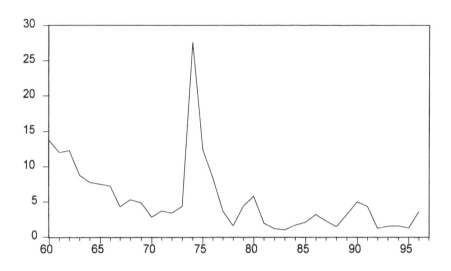

Figure 2.6   Gross International Reserves (in Months of Imports)

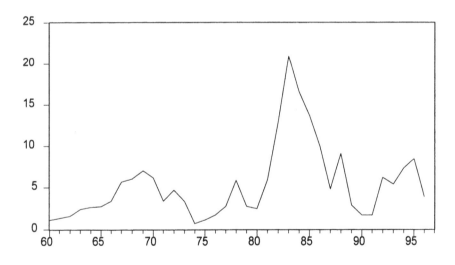

Figure 2.7   Ratio of M2 to International Reserves

Appendix 2.I

Intertemporal Solvency

Solvency deals with the ability of a country to generate sufficient net export surpluses (inclusive of services) in the future in order to repay the existing foreign liabilities. Milesi-Ferretti and Razin (1996) identified the inherent weaknesses of using this criterion to assess the external position of an economy. First, since current account balances reflect interactions among the savings and investment decisions of government, the domestic private sector and foreign investors, and since predicting the savings and investment behaviours of these three agents is quite problematic, there exists uncertainty in forecasting the ability of a country to generate sufficient future trade surpluses to repay the current debt obligations. Second, solvency does not distinguish between the ability and the willingness to pay and lend. From a theoretical perspective, though a country may be able to pay its current debt, it may not be politically feasible to divert a large amount of national output to debt servicing. Also, the lenders may not be willing to continue lending to an indebted country given the possibility of default.

Sustainability

The notion of sustainability goes somewhat beyond solvency. It poses the question: can current-account imbalances be sustained under the current policy (with government intertemporal budget constraints satisfied) without requiring a substantial change, or will they lead to a 'crisis'? If the answer is in the affirmative, the imbalance is sustainable. Therefore, the concept of sustainability imposes constraints on the current account imbalances in addition to those imposed by pure intertemporal solvency. We should note the inherent weaknesses of using macroeconomic indicators to assess the external position of a country. First, it is non-structural and, as a result, cannot be used to quantitatively assess the relative forecasting power of these indicators. Second, the indicators for assessing external imbalances could possibly lose their value to predict external crises once market participants and governments begin to incorporate them into their decision-making processes. This chapter and Chapter 6 use macroeconomic and structural indicators to complement the results observed from the intertemporal model to assess the excessiveness of the Nigerian current account deficits.

Excessiveness

The concept of excessive current account deficits expresses the deviation of the actual current account balance from an optimal or benchmark current account. The difference between the actual and optimal balance can be used to examine how close a given path of current account imbalances may be to unsustainability.

Examining the excessiveness of recurring or persistent current account deficits requires a formal model. The intertemporal models of the current account can be used for this purpose. These models in their simplest forms derive their conclusions from consumption-smoothing behaviour. They imply that unanticipated temporary declines in output in a small open economy will produce deterioration in the current account balance.

The assumptions used to derive the optimal current account balance are fundamental in determining the excessive current account balance. Assumptions behind the derivation of the optimal balance include: unrestricted access to the international capital markets and consumption depending on permanent income. These assumptions impact upon the derivation of the optimal current account.

External Crisis

Assessing the solvency, sustainability and excessiveness of the external position of a country is a means to an end, not an end in itself. There are several reasons for using these three criteria to determine the external position of a country. One of these is to determine whether the economy under consideration is likely to experience external crisis or not. The notion of external crisis employed in the present analysis could take the form of an exchange rate crisis (Frankel and Rose, 1996), an exchange rate crisis combined with a loss of reserves by the monetary authorities (Kaminsky, Lizondo and Reinhart, 1998) or a foreign debt crisis.[11] A debt crisis might arise from an inability to obtain further international financing or to meet repayments or from an actual default on debt obligations. A sustainable current account deficit is, therefore, one that can be sustained without experiencing any of these forms of external sector crises.

---

[11] Frankel and Rose (1996) define a currency crash as a nominal exchange rate depreciation of at least 25 percent. Kaminsky, Lizondo, and Reinhart (1998), on the other hand, perceive a currency crisis as a situation where a weighted average of monthly percentage change depreciations in the exchange rate and monthly percentage declines in reserves exceeds its mean by more than three standard deviations.

Data Appendix 2.II The Structure of Production (1960-97) (in percentages)

	Agriculture	Crude Petroleum	Manufact.	Construct.	Services	Utilities
1960	64.1	1.2	4.8	4.0	25.6	0.3
1961	62.2	1.8	5.2	4.2	26.3	0.3
1962	61.8	2.1	5.7	4.4	25.6	0.4
1963	61.5	2.1	6.0	4.2	25.7	0.5
1964	58.7	2.7	6.1	4.4	27.6	0.5
1965	55.4	4.8	7.0	5.2	27.1	0.5
1966	51.9	6.9	7.4	5.3	27.1	0.6
1967	52.7	6.4	7.4	5.3	27.5	0.7
1968	52.6	3.4	7.9	4.6	30.9	0.6
1969	47.5	8.1	8.2	5.2	30.3	0.7
1970	44.6	12.0	7.5	6.3	29.0	0.6
1971	42.0	15.1	6.5	7.5	28.3	0.6
1972	40.0	16.8	7.6	8.5	26.4	0.7
1973	37.6	22.9	7.9	6.7	24.3	0.6
1974	25.1	33.3	3.6	7.2	30.5	0.3
1975	25.6	22.3	5.6	8.7	37.5	0.3
1976	23.0	25.5	5.5	9.8	35.9	0.3
1977	23.4	25.3	5.0	9.6	36.4	0.3
1978	23.7	24.7	7.0	9.1	35.1	0.4
1979	21.9	27.5	9.1	7.6	33.4	0.5
1980	20.7	31.0	8.4	7.6	31.8	0.5
1981	20.5	26.3	9.8	7.9	34.9	0.6
1982	25.7	20.9	11.4	6.7	34.6	0.7
1983	28.7	18.6	11.2	6.2	34.4	0.9
1984	35.7	15.8	9.5	1.7	36.6	0.7
1985	35.0	16.5	10.7	1.8	35.3	0.7
1986	36.3	12.0	11.5	2.4	37.2	0.6
1987	36.7	24.1	6.8	2.0	30.0	0.5
1988	40.6	21.2	7.5	1.7	28.6	0.4
1989	31.3	35.7	5.3	1.7	25.5	0.5
1990	32.7	33.7	5.5	1.7	25.9	0.5
1991	30.4	37.7	5.9	1.5	24.0	0.4
1992	26.7	47.0	4.8	1.1	20.1	0.3
1993	33.5	35.7	5.6	1.2	23.8	0.2
1994	38.3	25.0	6.9	1.1	28.4	0.2
1995	31.6	40.5	5.4	0.7	21.7	0.1
1996	30.7	43.7	4.8	0.6	20.1	0.1
1997	33.6	39.0	5.1	0.7	21.6	0.1

Sources: Adapted from Oshikoya (1990) for 1960-86 data.
Central Bank of Nigeria: Statistical Bulletin (1998) for 1987-97 data.

Chapter 3

The Intertemporal Model of the Current Account: An Introduction

Introduction

This chapter presents an introduction to the present value model of the current account (PVMCA). This chapter has six main sections. Section 3.1 is a review of the literature on the earlier versions of the intertemporal approach to modeling the current account. Section 3.2 deals with empirical investigations of these earlier theoretical intertemporal models of the current account. The empirical results from estimating the PVMCA are reviewed in section 3.3. Section 3.4 examines the assumptions of the intertemporal models of the current account and their applicability to the Nigerian and Ghanaian economies. Section 3.5 concludes the chapter with a review of the existing literature on current account determination in Nigeria and Ghana.

3.1 Seminal Works on the Intertemporal Model of the Current Account

Intertemporal analyses of the current account became an active area of research in the early 1980s. These models of current account determination are based upon the permanent-income or life cycle hypothesis. Earlier theoretical intertemporal approaches to current account determination can be broadly divided into four groups.

The first group focused on establishing the major factors underlying international capital flows (Buiter, 1981; Obstfeld, 1986; Stockman and Svensson, 1987). These studies postulated that countries' differing preferences are the major factor underlying international capital flows, and consumption tilting, which depends among other factors, on the difference between the subjective discount factor and the world interest rate, can be important in explaining the behavior of the current account. In addition, the desire to smooth consumption is be an explanatory variable that must be taken into consideration in modeling the current account.

The second group emphasized the impact of changes in the terms of trade on the current account (Obstfeld, 1982; Svensson and Razin, 1983; Persson and Svensson, 1985). The major conclusion of these studies is that the responsiveness of the current account balance to changes in the terms of trade depends on whether such changes are anticipated or not and whether they are temporary or permanent. This group indicates that terms of trade changes need to be incorporated into modeling of the current account.

The third group examined the impact on the current account of temporary and permanent changes in government expenditures (Sachs, 1982). According to Sachs, when agents face an intertemporal budget constraint, a decision to alter current indebtedness implies changes in future consumption possibilities, with the result that a change will be based on expectations of the entire future path of key variables and current variables. Using a continuous time model, he showed that temporary and permanent shocks to government expenditures have different impacts on the current account. Temporary disturbances affect the current account balance through their impact on the optimal intertemporal consumption path of households. This is not the case with permanent changes.

The fourth group used an intertemporal framework to examine the optimal time path of consumption and external borrowing (Dornbusch, 1983; Hercowitz, 1986). These studies provided a framework that used the current account balance as an input into the derivation of the optimal time profile of external liabilities.

These studies served as theoretical foundations for empirical investigations of the intertemporal models of the current account. The literature on the early empirical investigations of these models is reviewed in the next section.

3.2 Early Tests of Intertemporal Current Account Models

Most structural time-series studies of the intertemporal approach to the current account essentially test implications of (3.1). Based on this equation, the current account depends on deviations of output, government spending, and investment from their permanent levels when the subjective discount factor equals the world market interest rate.

$$CA_t = (Y_t - \tilde{Y}_t) - (G_t - \tilde{G}_t) - (I_t - \tilde{I}_t) \qquad (3.1)[1]$$

Y_t, G_t and I_t represent output, government expenditures, and investment respectively. The ~ on a variable represents its permanent value. The central implication of the intertemporal approach is embodied in (3.1).

Most of the econometric tests of the implication of (3.1) were conducted for developed countries. Early econometric tests of the intertemporal approach, as represented by this equation, include those by Ahmed (1986), Johnson (1986) and Roubini (1988). Their major focus was to examine the relative impact on the current account of temporary and permanent changes in government expenditures. Based on the intertemporal approach, a one-unit permanent increase in government

---

[1]   The derivation of (3.1) is presented in Chapter 4.

expenditures produces an associated one-unit permanent reduction in private consumption, but no effect on the current account. However, given consumption smoothing, a temporary change in government consumption has no impact on private consumption but affects the current account significantly. These studies shared a common econometric methodology: instrumental variables and non-linear estimation. Despite some differences in the tests of the life-cycle hypothesis of the current account, as noted in Otto (1992), they all found some support for some of the predictions of this model.

Ahmed (1986) studied the determinants of the United Kingdom's trade balance for the period 1900 to 1980. He found that changes in temporary government spending had a larger impact on the balance of trade than permanent changes. However, the study had difficulty in decomposing actual government expenditures into temporary and permanent components.

Johnson (1986) focused on Canada over the 1952-76 period. The author used instrumental variable techniques suggested by Hayashi (1982). The paper identified consumption smoothing and the stance of fiscal policy as the major determinants of the current account.

Roubini (1988) used the OECD data set to examine the validity of the intertemporal approach. He derived a model of the current account that is based upon the joint assumptions of consumption smoothing by private agents and tax smoothing by the fiscal authority. By combining the two optimization problems, Roubini obtained the relationship between the current account on the one hand and the budget deficit, private investment and transitory change in output on the other. He concluded that empirical tests of the model for a sample of 18 OECD countries presented good evidence that international capital markets are widely integrated and that the 'Feldstein-Horioka puzzle' might be explained by the important role of fiscal deficits in the determination of the current account and saving behavior. Budget deficits and investment shared one-to-one negative associations with current account balances in most of the countries considered.

This book, along the lines of Otto (1992) focuses on the implications of the present-value model, which links today's current account to the expected future changes in the economy's net output. This model in its simplest form derives its conclusions from consumption smoothing behavior. It implies that an unanticipated temporary fall in output in a small open economy will produce deterioration in the current account balance. This approach has its origin in Campbell and Shiller's (1987) seminal work on the relationship between current saving and the expected change in labor income. Campbell (1987) showed that the standard rational-expectations consumption function has the implication that consumers will 'save for a rainy day': saving will increase when there is expectation of a decline in future labor income. The extension of this framework to current account determination can be found in Sheffrin and Woo (1990), Milbourne and Otto (1992), and Otto (1992). The equation describing this idea is:

$$CA_t = -\sum_{t=\tau+1}^{\infty}\left(\frac{1}{1+r^*}\right)^{t-\tau} E_\tau \Delta Q_t, \ \Delta Q_t = Q_t - Q_{t-1} \qquad (3.2)$$

CA_t is the current account balance in period t, r^* represents the world interest rate, Q_t is the net output (that is, the difference between gross domestic output, gross investment and government expenditure), E_T is the expectations operator and Δ represents the change operator.

This approach has a number of advantages over some of the previously used procedures for testing the validity of the intertemporal model of the current account. First, one advantage of this approach to testing the life-cycle model over some of the previous procedures, is that it uses a consistent treatment of the data's time series properties (Otto, 1992). A second advantage is that the structure of the PVMCA is such that the permanent change in a variable is assumed to be zero, so that the model is restricted to testing the effects of temporary changes in output, investment and government expenditure on the current account.

The next section focuses on empirical tests of the present value model of the current account.

3.3 Tests of the Present Value Model of the Current Account (PVMCA)

Testing the PVMCA involves the use of present value tests. This is an approach that fully utilizes the model's structure to derive testable hypotheses and make possible a consistent treatment of the data's time series properties. The simple present value model of the current account indicates that a country's current account deficit should be equal to the present value of the expected future increase in output, net of investment and government expenditures (this is the 'Present Value Model of the Current Account', or PVMCA). Therefore, a vector autoregression including the current account and output can be used to compute a forecast of this present value, based on the households' information set.

The implications of the PVMCA include: the stationarity of the optimal current account based on the stationarity of the change in net output and the equality between the optimal and actual current account. The implication of this theory that the VAR forecast of this present value should be equal to the current account can be tested using a Wald statistic, or by comparing the movements of the actual current account with those of the optimal current account. We review below various studies on developed and developing countries that used present value tests to assess the validity of the intertemporal model of the current account.

Sheffrin and Woo (1990) analyzed four countries (Belgium, Canada, Denmark and the United Kingdom) over the period 1955-85. Their findings were mixed. Net output was found to be a stationary variable only for the United Kingdom. In all cases, current accounts were found to be non-stationary variables. These results run contrary to the implications of the PVMCA, one of which is that the changes in the net output and current account are stationary variables. Based on the statistical restrictions of the model, which implies the equality of the actual and optimal current account, this implication was rejected for all the countries with the exception of Belgium. Sheffrin and Woo compared the variances of the actual and optimal current accounts. They found that the volatility of the actual current account exceeded that of the optimal account. One suggestion made by Sheffrin and Woo for improving the performance of the PVMCA was relaxation of the assumption of a single good. Another was to introduce a distinction between tradable and nontradable goods. These changes would make the real exchange rate an important variable in the model.

Milbourne and Otto (1992), using quarterly data on the Australian economy over the period 1959:3 to 1989:1, found that the Australian data were not consistent with the version of the permanent-income hypothesis used in their analysis. The model did not explain most of the larger sustained movements in the current account. The authors suggested introducing variable interest rates and relative prices (the terms of trade and exchange rates) into the PVMCA.

The objective of Otto (1992) was to examine the extent to which a model that is based solely upon 'consumption-smoothing' by forward-looking rational agents can explain the actual time series behavior of the economy's current account. The study found that the adopted version of the consumption-smoothing hypothesis failed to provide a statistically adequate explanation of the dynamic behavior of the USA or Canadian current account. Using quarterly data for both countries for the period 1950-88, they strongly rejected the restrictions implied by the present-value relationship for the current account. However, the unrestricted vector autoregression (VAR) showed a much closer relationship between the actual and forecast series for the USA than for Canada. Thus, the Canadian data provided virtually no support for the PVMCA. The author speculated that, for a small open economy like Canada's, the current account might be more affected by temporary changes in the resource prices and terms of trade. Therefore, the interest rates and terms of trade needed to be included in the PVMCA.

Ghosh (1995) considered five major industrial countries (Canada, Japan, Germany, United Kingdom and United states) over the period 1960:1–1988:4 (1962:1–1968:4 in the case of Germany). He used a quadratic utility function and a one-good model. He found some support for the PVMCA. The implication of the present value model that the optimal current account is a stationary variable was rejected only for Germany. The second implication, that changes in current account should help predict future changes in net output, was satisfied only for the United States. Moreover, a formal statistical test of the model based on the use of the Wald test, was rejected, except for the USA. However, the consumption-smoothing model of the current account performed extremely well in characterizing the direction and turning points of the current accounts of all five of the countries studied. In terms of the volatility of both the actual and predicted current account balances, there was no significant difference between the two in the case of the United States, while the actual balance was greater than the optimal one for the other four countries. One important conclusion drawn from this result was that the observed excess volatility of the actual current account balance relative to its optimal one could have emanated from short-term capital flows due to speculation in the foreign exchange markets.

Makrydakis (1999), using annual data over the period 1950-99 for Greece, found that optimal consumption smoothing did not take place over the sample period, suggesting that the existing restrictions to the free flow of capital were binding. His econometric analysis showed that the consumption-smoothing model was capable of explaining all major cyclical movements in Greece's current account but failed to account for the full magnitude of these fluctuations. Also, the stock of net foreign liabilities was found to have been on an unsustainable path following the 1989/90 balance of payments crisis; there was, however, clear evidence that this tendency had been gradually reversed during the last couple of years.

Ghosh and Ostry (1995) made the first attempt at applying the present-value approach to developing countries. They found that, across a large sample of developing countries, the level and volatility of net capital movements predicted by their consumption-smoothing model closely paralleled those in the data. The empirical results obtained for a number of African countries called for reformulating the theoretical basis of the PVMCA. In the first instance, the study found for African countries that the current account did not Granger-cause expected change in the net output. Also, the study discovered that the parameter differed frequently from its theoretically predicted value. Moreover, the joint test of the parameter restrictions implied by the model was rejected in five cases. In the cases in which the data did not reject the model (eight of thirteen), the parameters were imprecisely estimated.

As observed by Bergin and Sheffrin (2000), the results from empirical implementation of the PVMCA are mixed at best. While the simple intertemporal model has often been found to work fairly well for large countries, it, quite ironically, tends to fail for many small open economies, for which the assumptions of the theory should be most appropriate. A likely explanation is that external shocks, which are not considered in the simplest form of the intertemporal model, strongly affect small economies. External shocks will generally affect the small open economy via movements in the interest rate and the exchange rate. Using quarterly observations over the period 1960-96 for Australia, Canada and the United Kingdom, this study found that including the interest rate and the exchange rate improved the fit of the PVMCA compared to that in earlier studies: the model's predictions better replicated the volatility of current account data and better explained historical episodes of current account imbalances.

In line with Ghosh and Ostry (1995), this book suggests an extension of the intertemporal framework for modeling the behavior of the current account in Nigeria and Ghana. Analyzing the evolution of the current account requires a model that emphasizes the microeconomic underpinnings of decisions relating to savings and investments. Modeling the evolution of the current account in these two countries must reflect movements in the exchange rate, which is a manifestation of their macroeconomic indicators. Further, the changing terms of trade must be considered in modeling the behavior of their current account. When we take into consideration their political and macroeconomic evolution in recent decades, we are forced to include the possibility of their limited access to the international financial markets. Chapter 4 presents the theoretical foundation for the empirical investigations carried out in Chapter 5 for Nigeria and in Chapter 8 for Ghana.

The following section deals with the main assumptions of the present value model of the current account and the relevance of such assumptions in the context of the Nigerian economy.

3.4 Assumptions of the Intertemporal Model of the Current Account and the Applicability of the Model to the Nigerian Economy

One of the assumptions of the intertemporal model of the current account is that current consumption depends on permanent income. The PVMCA also assumes unrestricted access to the international financial market, so that any negative shocks to current output, with permanent income unchanged, will not affect current consumption but result in the accumulation of external liabilities. The important question investigated in this book is: how do these assumptions fare in developing economies such as those of Nigeria and Ghana?

Surveys by Gersovitz (1988) and Deaton (1989) provide several explanations as to why household consumption behavior in developing countries may be quite different from that of the developed countries. First, the members of the household in developing countries engage in resource sharing. Resource sharing implies that there is no need to save for the retirement years. The older generation supports the younger one by lowering their consumption. When the younger generation becomes older, they depend on the younger members of the household for their consumption expenditure. Thus, the life-cycle model of consumption with the assumption of 'hump' saving cannot explain consumption behavior of the household in most developing countries. Also, the household lives forever through resource transfers from one generation to another, so that the permanent income hypothesis may capture the actual experience in developing countries.

The second factor distinguishing the household consumption behavior of developed economies from that of the developed countries is the high volatility of income. This volatility partly arises from the agrarian base of most developing countries and changes in the terms of trade. In the face of uncertainty in income, there is a greater impetus to save for precautionary reasons, since this sort of uncertainty cannot be diversified through aggregate resource pooling (Deaton, 1989; Grimard, 1997). In addition, a typical household in developing countries is often liquidity constrained. This has the implication that when income is less than its permanent level, the household may not be able to borrow in order to maintain the same level of consumption.

The fact that the households in developing economies may not be able to smooth consumption in the face of negative income shocks constitutes a limitation of the application of the rational-expectation, permanent income consumption hypothesis. The theoretical framework developed in this book for current account determination accounts for this by allowing a possible asymmetry in access to the international financial market.

There are a number of other factors that favor the use of the permanent income hypothesis in developing economies, such as those of Nigeria and Ghana. A high number of households in Nigeria and Ghana, as in many developing countries, operate at near-subsistence income levels. This may strengthen the need to smooth consumption over time, so that a sudden increase in income, which is considered to be temporary, is likely to be saved.

In addition, Nigeria experienced a civil war over the 1967-70 period. This was a period of increasing real government expenditures due to the civil war. Since these expenditures would have been viewed as a temporary phenomenon, one would expect deficits in the current account in the course of this war. The Nigerian economy thus constitutes a natural framework for examining the validity of one of the implications of the intertemporal model of the current account, that is, an unexpected temporary increase in government expenditures generates a current account deficit.

Moreover, Nigeria and Ghana can be taken to be small open economies. For Nigeria, the export-GDP ratio increased from an annual average of 10 percent in the 1960s to 18 percent in the 1970s, 21 percent in the 1980s and 43 percent in the 1990s. For Ghana, the export-GDP ratio declined from 21 percent in the 1960s to 16 percent in the 1970s, and further to 12 percent in the 1980s before it increased to 28 percent in the 1990s. Therefore, the theoretical model of a small open economy should be applicable to current account determination in both Nigeria and Ghana.

Recurrent current account deficits are another feature of the Nigerian and the Ghanaian economies. In both, the external debt showed an increasing trend. The recurring current account deficits combined with the evolution of external debt shows the need for a framework for assessing the excessiveness of the current account balance. This book uses the PVMCA for this purpose.

As noted by Mwau and Handa (1995), a major point of contention in the economic literature on the developing economies is the extent to which the economic behavior of the government and the private sector can be adequately studied through the use of neoclassical models based on the assumption of rational optimizing agents. There are two choices available to researchers working on developing economies such as those of Nigeria and Ghana. The first choice is to work with a neoclassical framework and adjust it for the special features of developing economies. An alternative choice is to make use of a descriptive or *ad hoc* theoretical framework that is specific to the developing country being studied. This carries the implication that the results obtained from such analysis are only country-specific and cannot be used as a basis for policy formulation in other developing economies. This book follows the former approach and applies the intertemporal model of the current account to Nigeria and Ghana. However, its approach does take into consideration variables such as the terms of trade and the real exchange rate that seem to be important for them. It also assumes that economic agents in these two countries may have asymmetric access to international financial markets.

3.5 Existing Empirical Studies

Since the early 1960s, scholars in both countries have addressed the problem of the balance of payments and the major determinants of its current account balance. Examples of such studies on Nigeria include Olayide (1968), Osagie (1973), Ojo (1973), and Enunenwosu (1984), Fakiyesi and Umo (1995), Komolafe (1996), Egwaikhide (1997). The most notable studies on Ghana include Jebuni *et al.* (1994), Ghartey (1987), Harrigan and Oduro (1997) and Johnson (1970). These studies have their foundations in the traditional approaches to the current account and balance of payments: the elasticity, monetary, and absorption approaches[2]. While these studies identified the major determinants of the current account balance, they were static in nature, did not specify the process governing the formation of expectations and did not use the intertemporal framework to the current account as the basis of their analyses. Moreover, they cannot be used to analyze issues such as the role of the current account in assessing the extent of effective capital inflow into a country, and the excessiveness of current account deficits.

---

[2] Chapter 6 provides detailed information on these traditional approaches to current account determination.

Chapter 4

The Present Value Models of the Current Account

Introduction

This chapter develops the general theoretical framework for analysing the current account balance in an intertemporal environment. The major focus of each of the theoretical analyses presented in this chapter is to show the linkage between expected future changes in the economy's net output (gross domestic product less government and investment expenditures; all expressed in real terms) and the current account balance. Within the Present Value Model of the Current Account (hereafter PVMCA), a country's current account position will be in deficit (surplus) whenever net output is expected to rise (fall) over time. This has the implication that in the presence of high capital mobility, the current account deficit (which, from the balance of payments identity, is identical to net capital inflows less additions to foreign exchange reserves) should serve as a buffer to smooth consumption when there are shocks to output, investment, or government expenditures (Ghosh and Ostry, 1995). This perspective on current account determination resembles Campbell's (1987) position that, given the permanent-income hypothesis, household savings should equal the expected present value of future declines in household labour income.

This method of analysing the current account has a number of implications, which are derived in this chapter. These include the stationarity of the actual and optimal current accounts, and the equality of the variances of both the actual and optimal current account balances. Further, the PVMCA provides an alternative framework for assessing the degree of effective capital inflows into the Nigerian economy. Furthermore, the PVMCA can be used for assessing the excessiveness of current account deficits.

This chapter is divided into five parts. Section 4.1 develops the standard PVMCA that has been used by Ghosh and Ostry (1995) to test the validity of this approach for the Nigerian economy and other developing economies. This is referred to in this text as the 'Benchmark Theoretical Framework'. The Benchmark Theoretical Framework assumes one tradable good; as a result, there is no possibility of changes in the terms of trade and in the real exchange rate impacting upon the current account. The benchmark framework also excludes any possible asymmetry in access to international financial markets.

One of the extensions of the benchmark PVMCA in section 4.2 allows for tradable and nontradable goods.[1] As a result, movements in the real exchange rate and the interest rate are allowed to impact upon the current account. As noted by Bergin and Sheffrin (2000), a small open economy may be strongly affected by external shocks. These external shocks generally impact through changes in the interest rate and the exchange rate. By explicitly incorporating changes in these two variables, we are able to capture two main channels through which external shocks are likely to affect the Nigerian economy, especially its current account.

Section 4.3 extends the PVMCA by incorporating the terms of trade into the framework developed in section 4.2. This extension represents the first attempt at incorporating changes in the terms of trade in the PVMCA. As noted by Khan and Knight (1983), Nyatepe-Coo (1993) and other studies, transitory shifts in the terms of trade are crucial for the current account. Consequently, there is a need to factor changes in the terms of trade into the PVMCA. This chapter modifies the benchmark PVMCA to incorporate the impact of changes in the terms of trade on the consumption-based real interest rate, the consumption path and the current account.

Apart from incorporating changes in the terms of trade into the PVMCA, another theoretical contribution of this book is the inclusion of asymmetry in access to the international financial markets, after taking into consideration changes in the interest rate, the exchange rate and the terms of trade. To this end, the theoretical framework in section 4.3 is further extended in section 4.4 to accommodate asymmetry in access to the international financial market.[2] This asymmetry is postulated to emanate from political instability with consequent macroeconomic instability. Specifically, we assume that economic agents in Nigeria are constrained from responding to a temporary reduction in net output because they are unable to fully access external financial markets so as to smooth their consumption. However, they are able to fully respond to a temporary increase in net output, that is, there are no restrictions on capital outflows to smooth consumption. This extension is necessary since the benchmark PVMCA assumes unrestricted access to the international financial market.

While we have made various modifications and extensions to ensure that our theoretical framework reflects the features of the Nigerian economy, we have not incorporated precautionary savings (which result in higher saving in the face of high variability in income) into our analyses. Most empirical analyses delving into precautionary saving behaviour have assumed constant absolute risk aversion (CARA). However, the CARA utility function, despite its analytical tractability, is

---

[1]   Bergin and Sheffrin (2000) made the first attempt at incorporating changes in the interest and exchange rates in the PVMCA. However, this book will be the first attempt at empirical implementation of their theoretical framework for the Nigerian economy.

[2]   This is the first time that a PVMCA with changes in interest rate, exchange rate and terms of trade will account for possible asymmetry in access to international financial market. This book makes another contribution in postulating a simple and direct way for testing this asymmetry.

plagued by several uninteresting properties (see Carroll and Samwick, 1995; Handa, 2000, p. 116). To avoid the problems associated with the use of the CARA utility function, others have used the constant relative risk aversion (CRRA) utility function. However, such studies have had to assume one good: with more than one good, CRRA will not allow a closed form approximation relating changes in more than one good to income uncertainty. In the current context, there are a number of interesting issues that we want to capture, such as the effects on the current account of changes in the interest rate, exchange rate, and terms of trade. To achieve this, we have to go beyond the assumption of only one good, so that the incorporation of precautionary saving had to be left out of our analysis.

4.1 The Theoretical Framework of the Benchmark PVMCA[3]

Derivation of the Optimal Current Account Balance

Consider a small open economy that can lend and borrow at a constant real world interest rate, r^*, and produces a single tradable good, Y_t. The representative agent is assumed to have rational expectations. The infinitely lived household has the expected intertemporal utility function given by:

$$E_\tau U = E_\tau \left\{ \sum_{t=\tau}^{\infty} \beta^{t-\tau} [U(C_t)] \right\}, \quad U'(C_t) > 0 \; ; \quad U''(C_t) < 0 \; ; \quad 0 < \beta < 1$$

$$(4.1)$$

where β is the subjective discount factor; E is the expectation operator; U(.) represents the period or temporal utility function; and C_t represents the consumption of the single good in period t and $E_\tau U$ is the expected utility.

The assumption of a constant world interest rate is consistent with a one good model. However, it will be shown that when more than one good is assumed, given expected changes in the real exchange rate and the terms of trade, the interest rate will no longer be constant. Moreover, the assumption that the country is small in the international financial market implies that Fisherian separability is valid, so that investment should be chosen so as to maximize the economy's expected wealth, irrespective of the consumption profile. Consistent with this position,

---

[3] The contribution in this section is the demonstration of the use of dynamic optimization technique to establish optimal consumption. This optimal consumption is used in deriving the optimal current account. The existing literature on the present value model of the current account provides the utility function, the dynamic budget constraint and the final equation for the current account. However, this section provides clearly all the steps involved in showing that, in a simple intertemporal open economy model, the current account surplus equals the expected future decline of the present discounted value of net output.

Blanchard (1983) and Cooper and Sachs (1985) have demonstrated that investment should be undertaken until the marginal product of capital equals the world interest rate. This implies the separation of the consumption decision from that of the production decision.

The relationship between the net foreign asset and the current account balance is provided in (4.2):

$$B_{t+1} - B_t = r^* B_t + Y_t - C_t - G_t - I_t = CA_t \qquad (4.2)$$

where B_t is the net foreign assets, Y_t is the gross domestic product, C_t and G_t are respectively private and government expenditures, I_t is the sum of private and government investment, and CA_t is the current account balance, in period t.

Constraint (4.2) holds as an equality based on the assumption of non-satiation. By taking the expectation of (4.2) and by imposing a 'solvency condition' (*transversality condition* or *no Ponzi game condition*) to rule out the possibility of bubbles, iterating the dynamic budget constraint in (4.2) gives the intertemporal budget constraint facing the representative agent as:

$$E_\tau \left\{ \sum_{t=\tau}^{\infty} \left(\frac{1}{1+r^*} \right)^{t-\tau} Y_t + (1+r^*)B_\tau \right\} = E_\tau \left\{ \sum_{t=\tau}^{\infty} \left(\frac{1}{1+r^*} \right)^{t-\tau} (C_t + I_t + G_t) \right\}$$

$$(4.3)^4$$

Assuming that the competitive equilibrium of this model exists, we allude to the Second Welfare Theorem, which states that every Pareto efficient allocation is a Walrasian equilibrium (Mascollel *et al.*, 1995, pp. 551-558). The implication of this theorem is that the competitive equilibrium of this model is equivalent to the planner's solution. We use the planner's solution because of its simplicity. The social planner maximizes (4.1), subject to the constraint indicated in (4.3).

---

[4] Rewrite (2) as:
$$(1+r^*)B_t = C_t + G_t + I_t - Y_t + B_t$$
By shifting the last equation forward by one period and dividing through by $(1+r^*)$, we have:
$$B_{t+1} = \frac{C_{t+1} + G_{t+1} + I_{t+1} - Y_{t+1}}{1+r^*} + \frac{B_{t+2}}{1+r^*}$$
The equation above can now be used to eliminate B_{t+1}:
$$(1+r^*)B_t = C_t + G_t + I_t - Y_t + \frac{C_{t+1} + G_{t+1} + I_{t+1} - Y_{t+1}}{1+r^*} + \frac{B_{t+2}}{1+r^*}$$
As in the two-period case, $B_{t+T+1} = 0$. Also, $\mathrm{Lim}_{t \to \infty} (1/1+r)^T B_{t+T+1} = 0$.
By following this iterative substitution, successive values of B_{t+i} can be eliminated. This would transform the intertemporal budget constraint to (4.3).

Maximizing (4.1) subject to (4.3) gives the optimal path of consumption. To derive this, first rewrite (4.2) as:

$$C_t = Y_t + (1 + r^*)B_t - B_{t+1} - I_t - G_t \qquad (4.4)$$

Substituting (4.4) into (4.1), we have:

$$V(B_t) = E_\tau \left\{ \text{Max}(B_{t+1})_{t=\tau}^\infty \sum_{t=\tau}^\infty \beta^{t-\tau} \left[U(Y_t + (1 + r^*)B_t - B_{t+1} - I_t - G_t) \right] \right\}$$

$$(4.5)$$

The value function in (4.5) is continuous and differentiable. The optimisation problem in (4.1) has been transformed into one of choosing sequences of net foreign assets in (4.5). It is difficult to solve (4.5). To make it amenable to differentiation between two periods, we write it in the form of a Bellman equation:

$$V(B_\tau) = E_\tau \left\{ \text{Max} \begin{bmatrix} \left[U(Y_\tau + (1 + r^*)B_\tau - B_{\tau+1} - I_\tau - G_\tau) \right] + \\ \beta \text{Max} (B_{\tau+1})_{t=\tau}^\infty \sum_{t=\tau+1}^\infty \beta^{t-\tau} \left[U(Y_t + (1 + r^*)B_t - B_{t+1} - I_t - G_t) \right] \end{bmatrix} \right\}$$

$$(4.6)$$

Equation (4.6) can be re-expressed as:

$$V(B_\tau) = E_\tau \left\{ \text{Max}(B_{\tau+1}) \begin{bmatrix} U[Y_\tau + (1 + r^*)B_\tau - B_{\tau+1} - I_\tau - G_\tau] + \\ \beta \text{Max}(B_{\tau+1})_{t=\tau+1}^\infty \sum_{t=\tau+1}^\infty \beta^{t-(\tau+1)} \left[U(Y_t + (1 + r^*)B_t - B_{t+1} - I_t - G_t) \right] \end{bmatrix} \right\}$$

$$(4.7)$$

The second term on the right hand side of (4.7) has exactly the same form as (4.5), with B_{t+1} replacing B_t. Therefore:

$$V(B_\tau) = E_\tau \left\{ \text{Max} (B_{\tau+1}) [U(Y_\tau + (1 + r^*)B_\tau - B_{\tau+1} - I_\tau - G_\tau) + \beta V(B_{t+1})] \right\}$$

$$(4.8)$$

Equation (4.8) is often referred to as the functional equation or the Bellman Equation. The planner maximizes (4.8) by choosing the net foreign assets for the next period, given that the initial or current net foreign asset position was optimally chosen. By differentiating (4.8) with respect to B_{T+1}, and using the definition of current consumption in (4.4), we have:

$$-U'(C_t) + \beta\, V'(B_{T+1}) = 0 \tag{4.9}$$

Differentiating (4.8) with respect to B_T gives:

$$U'(C_T)(1+r^*) = 0 \tag{4.10}$$

Shifting (4.10) forward by one period, which is equivalent to differentiating with respect to B_{T+1}, produces:

$$(1+r^*)E_T\{U'(C_{T+1})\} = 0 \tag{4.11}$$

Substituting (4.11) into (4.9) yields:

$$U'(C_T) = (1+r^*)\beta E_T\{U'(C_{T+1})\} \tag{4.12}$$

The next step is to establish an equation for the consumption function, which will be used to derive the equation of the current account balance. We assume that $\beta = 1/(1+r^*)$[5]. Therefore, (4.12) becomes:

$$U'(C_T) = E_T U'(C_{T+1}) \tag{4.13}$$

We follow the literature in assuming a quadratic utility function, given by:

$$U(C) = C - \frac{\alpha_0}{2}C^2 \qquad \alpha_0 > 0 \tag{4.14}[6]$$

Differentiating (14) with respect to C yields:

$$U'(C) = 1 - \alpha_0 C \tag{4.15}$$

---

[5] This implies that the representative agent plans for a constant stream of consumption, and that consumption tilting is zero.

[6] Using the quadratic utility function implies that consumption is determined according to the certainty equivalence principle. However, this cannot be considered to be a rational basis for decisions. Despite the fact that this utility function provides us with a closed form solution for the consumption function, it has the inherent weaknesses of the marginal utility of consumption becoming negative (Handa, 2000, pp.120). Also, there are no additional benefits from precautionary savings since the third derivative of the utility function is zero. An isoelastic period utility function is used in other derivations in order to deal with the weaknesses of the quadratic utility function.

Substituting (4.15) into the Euler equation (4.13) produces:

$$(1 - \alpha_0)C_\tau = (1 - \alpha_0)E_\tau C_{\tau+1}$$

$$E_\tau C_{\tau+1} = C_\tau \qquad\qquad (4.16)$$

Equation (4.16) represents Hall's (1978) conclusion that consumption follows a random walk *(the martingale process)*. This has the implication that the expected value of C_{t+1}, conditional on all available information, is C_t. Noting that, for any $t > T$:

$$E_\tau C_t = E_\tau C_{t-1} = E_\tau C_{t-2} = ... = E_\tau C_{\tau+1} = C_\tau \qquad\qquad (4.17)$$

Therefore, substituting C_t for $E_T C_t$ in the expected-value budget constraint and rearranging yields:

$$\sum_{t=\tau}^{\infty} \left(\frac{1}{1+r^*}\right)^{t-\tau} C_t = E_\tau \left\{ (1+r^*)B_\tau + \sum_{t=\tau}^{\infty} \left(\frac{1}{1+r^*}\right)^{t-\tau} (Y_t - I_t - G_t) \right\}$$

$$(4.18)$$

From (4.18), the permanent income consumption function is specified by:

$$C^*_t = \frac{r^*}{1+r^*} \left[(1+r^*)B_\tau + \sum_{t=\tau}^{\infty} \left(\frac{1}{1+r^*}\right)^{t-\tau} E_\tau (Y_t - G_t - I_t) \right]$$

$$(4.19)^{[7]}$$

The open economy rational expectations consumption function is given by (4.19). As in Hall (1988), planned consumption is constant but actual consumption will change as the stochastic processes in the economy evolve. Substituting (4.19) into (4.2) produces the optimal current account balance:

$$CA^*_\tau = Y_\tau + r^* B_\tau - \left\{ \frac{r^*}{1+r^*} \left[(1+r^*)B_\tau + \sum_{t=\tau}^{\infty} \left(\frac{1}{1+r^*}\right)^{t-\tau} E_\tau (Y_t - I_t - G_t) \right] \right\}$$
$$- I_\tau - G_\tau$$

$$(4.20)$$

---

[7] We use the condition that:

$$1 + \frac{1}{1+r^*} + \left(\frac{1}{1+r^*}\right)^2 + ... = \frac{1}{1 - \dfrac{1}{1+r^*}} = \frac{1+r^*}{r^*} = \sum_{t=\tau}^{\infty} \left(\frac{1}{1+r^*}\right)^{t-\tau}$$

Equation (4.20) can be rewritten as:[8]

$$CA_\tau{}^* = Y_\tau - \frac{r^*}{1+r^*}\sum_{t=\tau}^{\infty}\left(\frac{1}{1+r^*}\right)^{t-\tau}E_\tau Y_t + \frac{r^*}{1+r^*}\sum_{t=\tau}^{\infty}\left(\frac{1}{1+r^*}\right)^{t-\tau}E_\tau G_t$$

$$+ \frac{r^*}{1+r^*}\sum_{t=\tau}^{\infty}\left(\frac{1}{1+r^*}\right)^{t-\tau}E_\tau I_t - G_\tau - I_\tau$$

(4.21)

Equation (4.21) implies that:

$$CA^*_\tau = \left(Y_t - E_\tau \hat{Y}_\tau\right) - \left(I_t - E_\tau \hat{I}_\tau\right) - \left(G_\tau - E_\tau \hat{G}_\tau\right)$$

(4.22)

The basis of the intertemporal model of the current account is provided by (4.22): the current account serves as a buffer through which private agents can smooth consumption over time in response to temporary disturbances to output, investment, and government expenditures. A rise (fall) in the current output above (below) its expected permanent value leads to an improvement in the current account (a deterioration), reflecting consumption smoothing. A temporary increase (decrease) in the current output above (below) its long run discounted average will induce individuals to accumulate (deplete) interest-bearing foreign assets as a way of smoothing consumption over future periods. Similarly, foreign borrowing will be used to finance profitable opportunities. This will be accomplished by borrowing abroad instead of reducing current consumption to finance such investment, so that the current account balance position will deteriorate. Finally, a temporary increase in government expenditures has the same effect as a temporary negative productivity shock: a higher current account deficit enables individuals to minimize the impact of such a shock in any particular period by spreading that impact over the entire future.

It is possible to write (4.22) in a more compact form, which will make it similar to the approach developed by Campbell (1987) for testing the permanent income hypothesis of consumption and to show that an expected positive change in net output in the future increases the current account deficit in the current period.

---

[8] Defining the relationship between the permanent value of a variable and its current value as:

$$\sum_{t=\tau}^{\infty}\left(\frac{1}{1+r^*}\right)^{t-\tau}\hat{Z}_\tau = \sum_{t=\tau}^{\infty}\left(\frac{1}{1+r^*}\right)^{t-\tau}Z_t$$

Therefore, the permanent value of Z is given by:

$$\hat{Z}_\tau = \frac{r^*}{1+r^*}\sum_{t=\tau}^{\infty}\left(\frac{1}{1+r^*}\right)^{t-\tau}Z_t$$

[See Obstfeld and Rogoff (1996) p.74, for this definition of a permanent variable].

For this compact form, we define net output as gross domestic output, less gross investment and government expenditures. That is:

$$Q_t \equiv Q_t - I_t - G_t \tag{4.23}$$

Based on this definition, (4.22) takes the simple form:

$$CA^*_{_T} = Q_t - E_{_T}\hat{Q}_t. \tag{4.24}$$

The permanent value of the net output, $\hat{Q}_t$, can be written as:

$$\hat{Q}_t = \frac{r^*}{1+r^*}\sum_{t=T}^{\infty}\left(\frac{1}{1+r^*}\right)^{t-T}E_{_T}Q_t \tag{4.25}$$

Substituting (4.25) into (4.24) gives:

$$CA^*_{_T} = Q_t - E_{_T}\frac{r^*}{1+r^*}\sum_{t=T}^{\infty}\left(\frac{1}{1+r^*}\right)^{t-T}E_{_T}Q_t \tag{4.26}$$

Setting $\dfrac{1}{1+r} = \psi$, we can rewrite (4.26) as:

$$CA^*_{_T} = Q_t - (1-\psi)\sum_{t=T}^{\infty}\psi^{t-T}E_{_T}Q_t$$

$$= Q_t - E_{_T}\left[\sum_{t=T}^{\infty}\psi^{t-T}Q_t - \sum_{t=T}^{\infty}\psi^{t-T+1}Q_t\right]$$

$$= Q_t - Q_t - E_{_T}\left[\sum_{t=T+1}^{\infty}\psi^{t-T}Q_t - \sum_{t=T}^{\infty}\psi^{t-T+1}Q_t\right] \tag{4.27}$$

Note that:

$$\sum_{t=T}^{\infty}\psi^{t-T+1}Q_t = \sum_{t=T+1}^{\infty}\psi^{t-T}Q_{t-1}$$

Therefore, (4.27) can be re-expressed as:

$$CA^*_\tau = -E_\tau\left[\sum_{t=\tau+1}^{\infty}\psi^{t-\tau}Q_t - \sum_{t=\tau+1}^{\infty}\psi^{t-\tau}Q_{t-1}\right]$$

$$= -E_\tau\left[\sum_{t=\tau+1}^{\infty}\psi^{t-\tau}(Q_t - Q_{t-1})\right] \qquad (4.28)$$

The current account in the current period based on (4.28) is:

$$CA^*_\tau = -\sum_{t=\tau+1}^{\infty}\left(\frac{1}{1+r}\right)^{t-\tau}E_\tau(\Delta Q_t) \qquad (4.29)$$

From (4.29), temporary shocks lead to changes in the current account, and the extent of the movement in the current account depends on the persistence of the shock. A country will run a current account surplus only if it expects its net output to fall temporarily in the future. The analogy to household saving is illuminating: as Campbell has shown, an implication of the rational-expectations permanent-income model is that households save when they expect their future labour income to decline. In our model, net output plays the role of labour income and the current account plays the role of savings.

This approach to looking at the current account balance has a number of policy implications. In the first place, the fact that the economy is experiencing current account deficits may not necessarily be indicative of structural problems. A temporary increase in government expenditure, in investment, or a decline in productivity, is expected to generate current account deficits. This shows that there is no need on the part of the government to initiate policy measures – for example, a devaluation – to correct such current account deficits. Secondly, if the observed current account deficit reflects the consumption smoothing of private economic agents, the current account deficits will not result in the accumulation of foreign liabilities that are not sustainable. Finally, if indeed the current account acts as a buffer, this implies a high degree of capital mobility. Thus, the PVMCA can be used to assess the degree of effective capital inflows into the country.

The Testable Implications of the Benchmark Theoretical Framework

The first implication of (4.29) is the stationarity of the optimal current account, CA_t^*. From (4.29), if the change in net output (ΔQ_t) is a stationary variable (i.e., I (0)), then the optimal current account CA^*_t must also be stationary in levels, since it is a linear combination of I (0) variables. The stationarity of CA^*_t, conditional on the stationarity of ΔQ_t, constitutes a relatively weak implication of the present value model (Otto, 1992). This implication can be tested using the Augmented

Dickey-Fuller (ADF) unit root test (see Said and Dickey, 1984) and the Phillips-Perron unit-root test (see Phillips and Perron, 1988).

The second implication of (4.29) is that of the equality between the actual and optimal current accounts. From (4.29), creating the optimal current account series requires estimating the present value of the expected change in net output, where the expectation is conditional on the information set used by economic agents. This is an uphill task: the information set on the basis of which agents forecast future values of the variables contained in net output is generally unknown to the researcher. However, precise knowledge of the content of information utilized by the agent is not needed. This is because, as Campbell and Shiller (1987) have shown in a different context, the current account itself reflects all the information available to agents for forecasting these variables. Indeed, under the null hypothesis of equation (4.29), the current account should itself incorporate all consumers' information on future net output changes.

Consumers' forecast of the change in net output (ΔQ_t) for $t > \tau$ is based on a p-order vector autoregression (VAR) model. Setting, for ease of exposition, $p = 1$,[9] this model is:

$$\begin{bmatrix} \Delta Q_t \\ CA_t \end{bmatrix} = \begin{bmatrix} \psi_{11} & \psi_{12} \\ \psi_{21} & \psi_{22} \end{bmatrix} \begin{bmatrix} \Delta Q_{t-1} \\ CA_{t-1} \end{bmatrix} + \begin{bmatrix} V_{1t} \\ V_{2t} \end{bmatrix} \tag{4.30}$$

where V_{1t} and V_{2t} are errors with a conditional mean of zero and where ΔQ_t and CA_t are now expressed as deviations from unconditional means, so that only the dynamic restrictions of the present value model of the current account are tested (see Campbell, 1987; Campbell and Shiller, 1987;, Otto, 1992; and Ghosh, 1995). Equation (4.30) is used to forecast the expected value of ΔQ_t in (4.29). Taking the expectation of (4.30) yields:

$$E_\tau \begin{bmatrix} \Delta Q_t \\ CA_t \end{bmatrix} = \begin{bmatrix} \psi_{11} & \psi_{12} \\ \psi_{21} & \psi_{22} \end{bmatrix}^{t-\tau} \begin{bmatrix} \Delta Q_\tau \\ CA_\tau \end{bmatrix} \tag{4.31}$$

In (4.31) we use the condition that $E_t[X_{t+j}] = \Psi^j X$; $E(V_{1t}) = E(V_{2t}) = 0$; and $\Psi =$ matrix $[\psi_{ij}]$. By pre-multiplying (4.31) by the 1x2 vector [1 0], we have:

$$E_\tau \Delta Q_t = \begin{bmatrix} 1 & 0 \end{bmatrix} \begin{bmatrix} \psi_{11} & \psi_{12} \\ \psi_{21} & \psi_{22} \end{bmatrix}^{t-\tau} \begin{bmatrix} \Delta Q_\tau \\ CA_\tau \end{bmatrix} \tag{4.32}$$

---

[9] It is straightforward to generalize this expression for higher order VARs by writing a pth-order VAR in the first order form [see Otto (1992)]. The derivations here follow Obstfeld and Rogoff (1996).

Let **I** be a 2x2 identity matrix, Substituting (4.32) into (4.29) yields:

$$CA^*_\tau = -[1 \ \ 0]\left[(1+r^*)^{-1}\Psi\right]\left[I - (1+r^*)^{-1}\Psi\right]^{-1}\begin{bmatrix}\Delta Q_\tau \\ CA_\tau\end{bmatrix}$$

$$= [\Phi_{\Delta Q} \ \ \Phi_{CA}]\begin{bmatrix}\Delta Q_\tau \\ CA_\tau\end{bmatrix} \qquad\qquad (4.33)^{10}$$

Equation (4.33) is the predicted or optimal current account that will be compared with the actual current account data. Therefore, to evaluate the model statistically, we have to test the restriction that $[\Phi_{\Delta Q} \ \Phi_{CA}] = [0 \ 1]$ in (4.33). This necessitates the use of the delta method to calculate a χ^2 statistic for the hypothesis that $k = \Phi_{\Delta Q} \ \Phi_{CA}] = [0 \ 1]$. Let g represent the difference between the actual k and the hypothesized value. Then, $g\left[(\partial k/\partial\psi)V(\partial k/\partial\psi)'\right]^{-1}g$ will be distributed chi-squared with two degrees of freedom, where V is the variance-covariance matrix of the VAR parameters, and $(\partial k/\partial\psi)$ is the matrix of derivatives of the k vector with respect to these parameters.

The third implication of (4.29) under the null is the equality of the variances of the actual current account and the optimal current account. If this is found to be valid, then the Nigerian economy can be considered as receiving sufficient capital flows to ensure consumption smoothing. On the other hand, a lower variance of the optimal current account balance than the actual one would be indicative of excessive speculation. A higher variance would suggest less capital mobility, since this would imply that a shock to either saving or investment does not result in corresponding movement of the current account balance.

The last implication of (4.29) is the stationarity of the actual current account balance. Given the null of equality between the actual and optimal current accounts, the optimal current account is an I (0) process; hence, the actual current account must also be an I (0) process.

The implications of the PVMCA to be tested are:

- The stationarity of the optimal current account is due to the stationarity of the change in net output.
- There is equality between the optimal and actual current account.
- There is equality of variances of the optimal and current accounts.
- The stationarity of the optimal current account implies the stationarity of the actual current account.

---

[10] The expression in (4.33) is valid as long as the infinite sum in (4.29) converges, which it will if the variables in the VAR are stationary.

4.2 The PVMCA with a Consumption-based Interest Rate

A likely explanation of the mixed performance of the simple intertemporal current account in small open economies, as mentioned in Chapter 3, is the omission of external shocks that are likely to significantly affect these economies. It is important to incorporate those shocks that emanate from a country's larger neighbours or the world in general, rather than to focus exclusively on shocks arising from the domestic economy, as is the case with the benchmark PVMCA presented in the preceding section. As individuals may adjust consumption and saving behaviour in response to changes in the real interest rates, countries may also adjust their current account in response to movements in the world real interest rate. For example, a sudden increase in the interest rate that worsens the net factor payment position may influence the government to reduce its consumption expenditures in order to achieve a target current position.

Furthermore, Dornbusch (1983) has demonstrated that an anticipated rise in the relative price of tradable goods can raise the cost of borrowing from abroad when interest is paid in units of these goods. Therefore, real exchange rate movements can impact upon the intertemporal allocation of consumption, with a consequent impact on the current account position, similar to the effect of changes in the interest rate. In addition to these intertemporal effects, by inducing substitution between tradable and nontradable goods at any point in time, exchange rate changes can also have intratemporal effects. In recognition of these, we relax the assumptions of one tradable good. The introduction of tradable and nontradable goods creates a mechanism through which exchange rate movements can make an impact upon the current account.

The presentation in this chapter follows the lead of Campbell and Mankiw (1989) in their work on consumption, Huang and Lin (1993) in their work on fiscal deficits, and Bergin and Sheffrin (2000) in their work on the PVMCA.

Derivation of the Optimal Consumption

Consider a small open economy that can lend and borrow at a variable real world interest rate, r*. The economy produces both tradable and nontradable goods. The infinitely lived household maximizes the lifetime utility function given by (4.35) subject to the dynamic budget constraint (4.36).

$$E_\tau U = E_\tau \left\{ \sum_{t=\tau}^{\infty} \beta^{t-\tau} \left[U(C_{Tt}, C_{NTt}) \right] \right\}, \quad U'(C_t) > 0 \; ; \; U''(C_t) < 0 \; ; \; 0 < \beta < 1$$

$$(4.35)$$

$$B_{t+1} - B_t = r*_{t+1} B_t + Y_t - (C_{Tt} + P_t C_{NTt}) - G_t - I_t \qquad (4.36)$$

The variables are as defined in Section 4.1, except that they are now measured in terms of traded goods. C_T is the consumption of tradable goods and C_{NT} is the consumption of nontradable goods. P_t is the relative price of nontradable goods in terms of tradable goods. Assume that the temporal utility function is isoelastic and the allocation of expenditure between tradables and nontradables is in the form of a Cobb-Douglas function. That is:

$$U(C_{Tt}, C_{NTt}) = \frac{1}{1-\sigma}\left(C_{Tt}^{\alpha} C_{NTt}^{1-\alpha}\right)^{1-\sigma} \tag{4.37}$$

$$\sigma > 0, \ \sigma \neq 1, \ 0 < \alpha < 1$$

The representative agent maximizes (4.35) subject to the dynamic budget constraint (4.36). In carrying out this intertemporal exercise, we must first demonstrate that the dynamic budget constraint in (4.36) can be written as:[11]

$$P_t * C_t * = Y_t + (1 + r_{t+1}*)B_t - B_{t+1} - I_t - G_t \tag{4.38}$$

where $C_t * = C_{Tt}^{\alpha} C_{NTt}^{1-\alpha}$, is an index of total consumption. The consumption-based index, P_t*, is the minimum amount of consumption expenditure[12] $C_t = C_{Tt} + P_t C_{Tt}$ such that $C_t* = 1$. We can now rewrite (4.37) as:

$$U(C_t *) = \frac{1}{1-\sigma}(C_t *)^{1-\sigma} \tag{4.39}$$

The problems of choosing tradable and nontradable goods intertemporally in (4.35) and intratemporally in (4.37) have been transformed into one of choosing the composite consumption index $C*$. Solving for $C*$ from (4.38) and substituting into (4.35) we have:

$$V(B_t) = E_\tau \left\{ \text{Max} \sum_{t=\tau}^{\infty} \beta^{t-\tau} U\left[\frac{Y_t + (1 + r*_{t+1})B_t - B_{t+1} - I_t - G_t}{P_t *}\right]\right\} \tag{4.40}$$

----

[11] See Appendix 4.I for the derivation of (4.38). The derivation of the optimal consumption is based on the works of Dornbusch (1983) and Obstfeld and Rogoff (1996).

[12] This is the total consumption expenditure from the dynamic budget constraint in (4.36).

The procedures presented in equations (4.6) to (4.8) were used to derive the Euler equation. Following the same procedure for the utility function in (4.39) yields:

$$E_\tau \left[\beta (1 + r^*_{t+1}) \left(\frac{P_t^*}{P_{t+1}^*} \right) \left(\frac{C_t^*}{C_{t+1}^*} \right)^\sigma \right] = 1 \tag{4.41}$$

To ensure empirical implementation, we need to rewrite (4.41) in terms of consumption expenditure and the relative price of nontradable goods. To achieve this, we re-express (4.41) as:

$$E_t \left[\beta (1 + r_{t+1}) \left(\frac{P_t^* C_t^*}{P_{t+1}^* C_{t+1}^*} \right)^\sigma \left(\frac{P_t^*}{P_{t+1}^*} \right)^{1-\sigma} \right] = 1 \tag{4.42}$$

Rewrite (4.42) as:

$$E_t \left[\beta (1 + r_{t+1}) \left(\frac{C_t}{C_{t+1}} \right)^\sigma \left(\frac{p_t}{p_{t+1}} \right)^{(1-\sigma)(1-\alpha)} \right] = 1 \tag{4.43}$$

Assume joint log normality, constant variances and covariances for the gross real world interest rate $(1+r^*_{t+1})$, consumption growth rate $(\Delta c_{t+1} = \log C_{t+1} - \log C_t)$, and for the percentage change in the relative price of nontradable goods $(\Delta p_{t+1} = \log P_{t+1} - \log P_t)$.[13] Based on the assumption of lognormal distribution, (4.43) may be rewritten in a log-linearized form as[14]:

$$E_t \Delta c_{t+1} = \gamma E_t \left[r^*_{t+1} + \frac{1-\gamma}{\gamma} (1-\alpha) \Delta p_{t+1} \right]$$
$$+ \frac{1}{2} \left[\sigma_c^2 + \gamma^2 \sigma_r^2 + (1-\gamma)^2 (1-\alpha)^2 \sigma_p^2 + 2\gamma\gamma_{c,r} + 2(1-\gamma)(1-\alpha)\sigma_{c,p} + 2\gamma(1-\gamma)(1-\alpha)\sigma_{r,p} \right] \tag{4.44}$$

where $\gamma = 1/\sigma$ is the elasticity of intertemporal substitution.

---

[13] See Campbell *et al.* (1997, pp. 306-307), for the properties of a random variable that is conditionally lognormal distributed.

[14] Given the condition that the empirical implementation of the model will be based on de-meaned variables, the preference parameter, a constant, is dropped from equation (4.44).

Equation (4.44) assumes the approximation of log $(1+r^*_{t+1})$ as r^*_{t+1}. The first bracket on the right hand side of (4.44) specifies the consumption-based real interest rate, which is different from the world real rate of interest when there is an expected change in the real exchange rate. This is the own rate of interest on the consumption index C_t^*, and is denoted by $\hat{r}_t$. This rate of interest is no longer a constant and its movements are sensitive to expected changes in the real exchange rate. Therefore, the evolution of the optimal consumption profile is given by:

$$E_t \Delta c_{t+1} = \gamma E_t \hat{r}_{t+1}$$

where $\quad \hat{r}_t = r^* + \dfrac{1-\gamma}{\gamma}(1-\alpha)\Delta p_{t+1} + \text{constant}$ [15]   (4.45)

The relationship between the evolution of optimal consumption and the consumption-based interest rate, $\hat{r}_t$, is given by (4.45). The consumption-based real interest rate combines both the world interest rate r_t^* and the change in the relative price of nontradable goods. Previous empirical investigations of the intertemporal model of the current account emphasize a consumption profile where the expected change in consumption is zero: households try to smooth consumption over time by participating in the international financial markets. When the real interest rate is variable, as shown in (4.45), the representative consumer may decide to alter the path of consumption over time by increasing or decreasing consumption in some periods because of changes in the terms of borrowing and lending.

A change in the relative price of nontradable goods can have similar intertemporal effects as that of a change in the conventional interest rate. For example, an increase in the conventional real interest rate, r_t^*, makes current consumption more expensive in terms of foregone future consumption, and induces substitution toward future consumption with elasticity γ. Relating this scenario to the relative price of nontradable goods, if the price of nontradable goods is temporarily high and expected to fall, then the future repayment of a loan contracted in the current period in traded goods has a higher cost in terms of the consumption bundle than in terms of tradable goods alone. As a result, the consumption-based interest rate, $\hat{r}_t$ rises above the conventional interest rate, r^*. This induces a fall in the current total consumption expenditure by elasticity $\gamma(1-\alpha)$. Apart from this intertemporal substitution, a change in the relative price of nontradable goods also induces intratemporal substitution. In the event of a temporarily high relative price of nontradable goods, a household will substitute towards traded goods by the intratemporal elasticity, which is unity under the Cobb-Douglas specification. This increases total current consumption expenditure

---

[15] The constant term at the end of the expression will drop out of the empirical model when we later de-mean the consumption based interest rate using (4.45).

by elasticity $(1-\alpha)$. This intratemporal effect will dominate the intertemporal effect if the intertemporal elasticity, γ, is less than unity.

4.2.2 Log-Linearization of the Intertemporal Budget Constraint

The dynamic budget constraint in (4.36) can be re-written as:

$$CA_t = Y_t - I_t - G_t - (C_{Tt} + P_t C_{NTt}) + r^*_{t+1} B_t$$

$$= Q_t - C_t + r^*_{t+1} B_t \qquad (4.46)$$

where $Q_t \equiv Y_t - I_t - G_t$, and $C_t = (C_{Tt} + P_t C_{NTt})$. Define $R_{T,t}^*$ as the market discount factor for date T consumption, so that:

$$R_{T,t}^* = \frac{1}{\prod_{j=T+1}^{t}(1+r^*_j)} \qquad (4.47)^{16}$$

We sum over all periods of the infinite horizon, and impose the *no ponzi game* constraint as in Section 4.1. Combining this with (4.47), equation (4.46) becomes:

$$\sum_{t=0}^{\infty} E_0(R^*_t C_t) = \sum_{t=0}^{\infty} E_0(R^*_t Q_t) + B_0 \qquad (4.48)$$

Next, (4.48) is log-linearized using the Huang and Lin (1993) procedures. The first step in doing is to log-linearize the present value of net output. Define:

$$\Gamma_0 = \sum_{t=0}^{\infty} E_0(R^*_t Q_t) \qquad (4.49)$$

---

[16] This is necessary given the assumption of a variable interest rate. It replaces the usual

discount factor $\sum_{t=T}^{\infty}\left(\frac{1}{1+r^*}\right)^{t-T}$ under the assumption of a constant interest rate. Also,

$R_{T,T} = 1$; $R_{T,T+1} = \frac{1}{(1+r^*_{t+1})}$, and so on.

Appendix 4.II proves that (4.49) implies that:

$$q_0 - \phi_0 = \sum_{t=1}^{\infty} \rho^t \left(r_t^* - \Delta q_t \right) + \eta \qquad (4.50)^{17}$$

where $q_0 = \ln Q_0$, $\phi_0 = \ln \Gamma_0$, $\Delta q_t = q_t - q_{t-1}$; and η is a constant; ρ is a constant, slightly less than one and can be interpreted as the average value of $1 - Q/\Gamma$.

    The second step involves log-linearisation of the present value of current and future consumption:

$$X_0 = \sum_{t=0}^{\infty} E_0 \left(R_t * C_t \right) \qquad (4.51)$$

Using the procedures in Appendix 4.II, (4.51) implies that:

$$c_0 - x_0 = \sum_{t=1}^{\infty} \rho^t \left(r_t^* - \Delta c_t \right) + \eta \qquad (4.52)$$

where $c_0 = \ln C_0$; $x_0 = \ln X_0$; $\Delta c_t = c_t - c_{t-1}$; η is a constant; ρ is constant, slightly less than one, and can be interpreted as the average value of $(1 - C/X)$.

    Based on the same procedures, Appendix 4.II shows that the intertemporal budget constraint $\Gamma_0 = X_0 + B_0$ implies that:

$$x_0 - \phi_0 = \left(1 - \frac{1}{\Omega} \right) [b_0 - \phi_0] + k \qquad (4.53)$$

where $b_0 = \ln B_0$; Ω is constant, at (slightly) less than one, and can be interpreted as the average value of $1 - B/X$. k is a constant.

    Substituting for ϕ_0 and x_0 respectively from (4.50) and (4.52) into (4.53), produces the following log-linearized intertemporal budget constraint for the representative agent for $t \geq 0$:

$$-\sum_{t=1}^{\infty} \rho^t (\Delta q_t) \left[-\frac{1}{\Omega} \Delta c_t - \frac{\Omega - 1}{\Omega} r_t^* \right] = q_0 - \frac{1}{\Omega} c_0 + \frac{\Omega - 1}{\Omega} b_0 \qquad (4.54)$$

---

[17] Appendix 4.II provides the detailed derivation of this equation. The same procedure is used in transforming (4.51) and the entire intertemporal budget constraint.

Taking the expectation of (4.54), and using the optimal consumption profile in (4.45), equation (4.54) may be written as:

$$
-E_t \sum_{i=1}^{\infty} \beta^i \left(\Delta q_{t+i} \right) - \frac{\gamma}{\Omega} \hat{r}_{t+1} - \frac{\Omega - 1}{\Omega} r_t^* = q_t - \frac{1}{\Omega} c_t + \frac{\Omega - 1}{\Omega} b_t
$$

(4.55)

The right-hand side of (4.55) is similar to the definition of the current account in (4.46), except that its components are in log terms. We designate the transformed representation of the current account as CA**. This is the optimal current account balance when the interest rate is not constant and expected change in the real exchange rate or the relative price of nontradable goods is taken into consideration. We follow the convention of choosing the steady state around which we linearize to be the one in which net foreign assets are zero. In this case, $\Omega = 1$ and (4.55) can be formulated as:

$$
CA_t ** = -E_\tau \sum_{t=\tau+1}^{\infty} \beta^{t-\tau} \left(\Delta q_t - \gamma \hat{r}_t \right)
$$

(4.56) [18]

This condition stipulates that an expected increase in net output would produce a current account deficit in the current period as the representative agent smoothes consumption. Apart from the shocks emanating from the three components of the net output, (4.56) also implies that a fall in the consumption-based interest rate will lead to a deterioration in the current account position by inducing the representative household to increase consumption above its smoothed level. (4.56) augments equation (4.29) for the benchmark PVMCA in section 4.1 by the additional variable $\hat{r}_t$. Therefore, the restrictions implied by (4.56) can be tested using the framework described in section 4.1 but augmented with the additional variable, $\hat{r}_t$. This produces:

$$
\begin{bmatrix} \Delta Q_t \\ CA_t \\ \hat{r}_t \end{bmatrix} = \begin{bmatrix} \psi_{11} & \psi_{12} & \psi_{13} \\ \psi_{21} & \psi_{22} & \psi_{23} \\ \psi_{31} & \psi_{32} & \psi_{33} \end{bmatrix} \begin{bmatrix} \Delta Q_{t-1} \\ CA_{t-1} \\ \hat{r}_{t-1} \end{bmatrix} + \begin{bmatrix} V_{1t} \\ V_{2t} \\ V_{3t} \end{bmatrix}
$$

(4.57)

---

[18] This condition is similar to that of equation (4.29), except for the inclusion of the consumption-based interest rate and for the fact that the variables are in log form.

We need to determine the expected values of ΔQ_{t+i} and $\hat{r}_{t+i}$. To arrive at (4.57), we use the conditions $E_t [X_{t+j}] = \Psi^j X$, , $E (V_{1t}) = E (V_{2t}) = E (V_{3t}) = 0$, and Ψ= matrix $[\psi_{ij}]$. Therefore:

$$hz_t = -\sum_{t=\tau+1}^{\infty} \beta^{t-\tau}(g_1 - \gamma g_2)\Psi^{t-\tau} z_t \tag{4.58}$$

where $z_t, = (\Delta Q_t \, CA_t \, \hat{r}_t \,)'$, $g_1 = [1\ 0\ 0]$, $g_2 = [0\ 0\ 1]$, and $h = [0\ 1\ 0]$.[19] For a given z_t, the right hand side of the last equation can be expressed as:

$$CA_t{}^{**} = kz_t \tag{4.59}$$

where $k = -(g_1 - \gamma g_2)\beta\Psi(I - \beta\Psi)^{-1}$.

Equation (4.59) provides the model's prediction for the current account, consistent with the VAR and the restrictions of the intertemporal theory.

To evaluate the model, we have to test the hypothesis that $k = [0\ 10]$ in (4.59), so that $CA^{**}_t = CA_t$, by using the delta method to calculate a χ^2 statistic. Let k^* be the difference between the actual k and the hypothesized value. Then,

$k^{*\prime}\left((\partial k/\partial\Psi)V (\partial k/\partial\Psi)'\right)^{-1} k^*$ will be distributed chi-squared with 3 degrees

of freedom, where V is the variance-covariance matrix of the VAR parameters, and $(\partial k/\partial\Psi)$ is the matrix of derivatives of the k vector with respect to these parameters.

The major implications of the PVMCA when the interest rate is not constant and the expected change in the real exchange rate is incorporated into the model are:

- The stationarity of the optimal current account is due to the stationarity of the change in net output adjusted for the consumption based interest rate.
- There is equality between the optimal and the actual current account balances.
- There is equality of the variance of the optimal and the actual current accounts.
- The actual current account is stationary.

---

[19] Just as for the benchmark PVMCA, this can be generalized for a larger number of lags.

4.3 The PVMCA with a Consumption-Based Interest Rate and with Terms of Trade Changes

Allowing for changes in the terms of trade requires disaggregating the tradable goods into exportables and importables. It will be assumed that the exportable good is not consumed at home and that the goods consumed at home are importable and nontradable goods.[20]

The consumption-based interest rate and the world interest rate will differ from each other whenever the terms of trade (the relative price of importables) or the real exchange rate (the relative price of nontradables) is not expected to remain constant through time. Allowing for the consumption of importables and nontradables permits the incorporation of changes in the terms of trade, where the terms of trade are now the relative price of importables in terms of exportables, and the real exchange rate is the relative price of nontradables in terms of the price of exportables. This formulation is along the lines of Ostry and Reinhart (1992) and Ostry (1988).

Derivation of Optimal Consumption and Current Account

Consider a small open economy that can lend and borrow at a varying real world interest rate, r*, and consumes both importables and nontradable goods. The infinitely lived household maximizes the expected value of the lifetime utility function in (4.60), subject to the dynamic budget constraint in (4.61):

$$E_T U = E_t \left\{ \sum_{t=T}^{\infty} \beta^{t-T} \left[U(C_{mt}, C_{NTt}) \right] \right\}, \quad U'(C_t) > 0 \; ; \; U''(C_t) < 0 \; ; \; 0 < \beta < 1$$

(4.60)

$$\frac{P_t^m}{P_t^e} C_{mt} + \frac{P_t^n}{P_t^e} C_{NTt} = \frac{Y_t + (1+r^*)B_t - B_{t+1} - I_t - G_t}{P_t^e}$$

$$P_t^m C_{mt} + P_t^n C_{NTt} = Y_t + (1+r^*)B_t - B_{t+1} - I_t - G_t$$

$$P^*_t C^*_t = Y_t + (1+r^*)B_t - B_{t+1} - I_t - G_t \qquad (4.61)^{[21]}$$

The variables are as defined in Section 4.1 except that they are now measured in terms of exportable goods. C_{mt} is the consumption of imported goods

---

[20] In Nigeria, shifts in the terms of trade play an important role in the relative domestic demand for these two goods.

[21] We allude to the derivation in Appendix 4.I. Further details are provided in Appendix 4.III.

and C_{NTt} is the consumption of nontraded goods. The relative price of importables in terms of exportables is given by $P^t_m/P_e = P_{mt}$ (this is the case because exportable are the numeraire and their price is set to 1). The relative price of nontradable goods in terms of exportables is captured by $(P^t_n/P_e = P_{nt})$.

The intratemporal utility function is isoelastic and the allocation of expenditure between tradables and nontradables is in the form of a Cobb-Douglas function:

$$U(C_{mt}, C_{NTt}) = \frac{1}{1-\sigma}\left(C_{mt}^{\alpha} C_{NTt}^{1-\alpha}\right)^{1-\sigma} \tag{4.62}$$

Appendix 4.III derives the first-order conditions for this problem and uses them to derive the following optimal consumption profile:

$$E_t\left[\beta(1+r_{t+1})\left(\frac{C_t}{C_{t+1}}\right)^{\sigma}\left(\frac{p_{nt}}{p_{nt+1}}\right)^{(1-\sigma)(1-\alpha)}\left(\frac{p_{mt}}{p_{mt+1}}\right)^{\alpha(1-\sigma)}\right] = 1 \tag{4.63}$$

Equation (4.63) can be re-written as:

$$E_t\left[\beta^{\gamma}(1+r_{t+1})^{\gamma}\left(\frac{C_t}{C_{t+1}}\right)^{\gamma}\left(\frac{p_{nt}}{p_{nt+1}}\right)^{(\gamma-1)(1-\alpha)}\left(\frac{p_{mt}}{p_{mt+1}}\right)^{(\gamma-1)(\alpha)}\right] = 1 \tag{4.64}$$

where $\gamma = 1/\sigma$, the elasticity of intertemporal substitution. Based on the assumption of lognormal distribution, (4.64) may be rewritten in a log-linearized form as:[22]

$$E_t\Delta c_{t+1} = \gamma E_t\left[r^*_{t+1} + \frac{1-\gamma}{\gamma}(1-\alpha)\Delta p_{n_{t+1}} + \frac{1-\gamma}{\gamma}\alpha\Delta p_{m_{t+1}}\right] \tag{4.65}$$

---

[22] Given the condition that the empirical implementation of the model will be based on demeaned variables, the preference parameter is dropped from equation (4.66).

Therefore, the evolution of optimal consumption profile is given by:

$$E_t \Delta c_{t+1} = \gamma \, E_t \hat{r}_{t+1} \qquad\qquad (4.66)$$

where $\hat{r}_t = r^* + \dfrac{1-\gamma}{\gamma}(1-\alpha)\Delta p_{nt+1} + \dfrac{1-\gamma}{\gamma}\alpha\Delta p_{mt+1}$.

The difference between the evolution of consumption in (4.66) and that in (4.45) – which for the PVMCA without terms of trade – is the inclusion of changes in the terms of trade. All the restrictions derived in Section 4.2 for the earlier benchmark models are equally applicable here, but with the difference that the consumption based interest rate, $\hat{r}$, is now defined to include changes in the terms of trade. The optimal current account is given by:

$$CA_t^{***} = -E_\tau \sum_{t=\tau+1}^{\infty} \beta^{t-\tau}\left(\Delta q_t - \gamma \hat{r}_t\right) \qquad\qquad (4.67)$$

Equation (4.67) is similar to (4.56), except that (4.67) adjusts the consumption-based interest rate for changes in the terms of trade.

4.4 The PVMCA with Asymmetry in Access to the International Financial Markets

One of the weaknesses of the standard consumption-smoothing model of the current account is its assumption of unrestricted access to the international financial market. An important extension of the model would be to include asymmetry in access to the international financial markets: while private agents can easily lend abroad, it may be difficult for them to borrow abroad in the face of unanticipated negative shocks to net output. This may be a result of the perception of the lenders that the negative shock has reduced the ability of the private agents to pay back.[23]

We follow Callen and Cashin (1999) in allowing for asymmetric behaviour on the part of economic agents in their responses to temporary shocks to net output. However, while Callen and Cashin interpreted this asymmetric behaviour as resulting from capital controls imposed by the government, we perceive it in the current context as emanating from macroeconomic and political instabilities in an economy such as Nigeria's. Macroeconomic instability, for example, reduces the growth potential of the economy and thereby reduces the ability of private agents to repay back funds secured on the international financial

---

[23] This may be quite extreme as this implies that there is no change in the current account position in the face of negative external shocks. The best scenario would have been one where the capital inflow is insufficient to smooth consumption.

markets. International financial markets, anticipating this, may not be willing to lend to private agents in Nigeria to smooth consumption.

To implement the constrained model, the actual current account CA_t is decomposed into two main components as follows:

$$CA_t^h = D_t^h CA_t \text{ where } D_t^h = \begin{cases} 1 \text{ if } CA_t > 0 \\ 0 \text{ if } CA_t \leq 0 \end{cases}$$

$$(4.68)$$

$$CA_t^l = D_t^l CA_t \text{ where } D_t^l = \begin{cases} 1 \text{ if } CA_t < 0 \\ 0 \text{ if } CA_t \geq 0 \end{cases}$$

$$(4.69)$$

where CA_t^h, (CA_t^l) equals CA_t when CA_t is positive (negative); CA_t^h (CA_t^l))is zero otherwise. The variables ΔQ_t^h and ΔQ_t^l are defined similarly as:

$$\Delta Q_t^h = D_t^h \Delta Q_t \text{ where } D_t^h = \begin{cases} 1 \text{ if } \Delta Q_t > 0 \\ 0 \text{ if } \Delta Q_t \leq 0 \end{cases}$$

$$(4.70)$$

$$\Delta Q_t^l = D_t^l \Delta Q_t \text{ where } D_t^l = \begin{cases} 1 \text{ if } \Delta Q_t < 0 \\ 0 \text{ if } \Delta Q_t \geq 0 \end{cases}$$

$$(4.71)$$

In the PVMCA, an expected rise in output generates an increase in current consumption, so that, with a constant current income, it decreases saving. With unchanged investment, the current account balance deteriorates. However, with only partial access to the international financial market, the current account position will not be fully affected by the expected increase in output. Now suppose that the domestic economic agents can fully lend abroad. When agents expect a decline in their future output, they can reduce current consumption, thereby increasing saving, with a consequent improvement in the current account position. Therefore, in the presence of credit asymmetric access, the relationship between the net cash flow and current account takes two forms. If the postulate of asymmetry in the access to the international financial market is binding, then CA_t^h will Granger-cause future changes in net output, as defined by ΔQ_t^l. However, no Granger causality should be found between CA_t^l and ΔQ_t^h.

Another test of the appropriateness of the constrained consumption-smoothing model can be carried out by estimating the VAR system including the variables of interest. To do this, we can estimate a five-variable VAR of current and lagged changes in net output (ΔQ^h and ΔQ^l), current and lagged values of the actual current account ($C\hat{A}_t^h$ and $C\hat{A}_t^l$), and the consumption-based interest rate of the form:

$$
\begin{bmatrix}
\Delta Q_t^h \\
\Delta Q_t^l \\
CA_t^h \\
CA_t^l \\
\hat{r}_t
\end{bmatrix}
=
\begin{bmatrix}
\Psi_{11} & \Psi_{12} & \Psi_{13} & \Psi_{14} & \Psi_{15} \\
\Psi_{21} & \Psi_{22} & \Psi_{23} & \Psi_{24} & \Psi_{25} \\
\Psi_{31} & \Psi_{32} & \Psi_{33} & \Psi_{34} & \Psi_{35} \\
\Psi_{41} & \Psi_{42} & \Psi_{43} & \Psi_{44} & \Psi_{45} \\
\Psi_{51} & \Psi_{52} & \Psi_{53} & \Psi_{54} & \Psi_{55}
\end{bmatrix}
\begin{bmatrix}
\Delta Q_{t-1}^h \\
\Delta Q_{t-1}^l \\
CA_{t-1}^h \\
CA_{t-1}^l \\
\hat{r}_{t-1}
\end{bmatrix}
+
\begin{bmatrix}
V_{1t} \\
V_{2t} \\
V_{3t} \\
V_{4t} \\
V_{5t}
\end{bmatrix}
$$

(4.72)

From (4.72), the restrictions on the optimal current account (with asymmetry in access to the international financial market) are given by:

$$
hz_t = -\sum_{t=\tau+1}^{\infty} \beta^{t-\tau}(g_1 - \gamma g_2)\Psi^{t-\tau} z_t
$$

(4.73)

where $z_t = (\Delta Q_t^h\ \Delta Q_t^l\ CA_t^h\ CA_t^l\ \hat{r}_t)'$, $g_1 = [1\ 1\ 0\ 0\ 0]$, $g_2 = [0\ 0\ 0\ 0\ 1]$, and $h = [0\ 0\ 1\ 1\ 0]$. (This can also be generalized for a larger number of lags). These restrictions are consistent with the joint null hypotheses of consumption smoothing and the absence of credit constraints. This restriction implies that movements of the actual current account reflect those of the optimal current account. The alternative hypothesis is that asymmetry in access to the international financial markets is binding, so that the restrictions captured in h are not valid.

For a given z_t, the right hand side of (4.73) can be expressed as:

$$
CA_t{}^{****} = kz_t
$$

(4.74)

where $k = -(g_1 - \gamma g_2)\beta\Psi(1-\beta\Psi)^{-1}$. CA_t^{****} is the optimal current account balance in the presence of asymmetry in access to the international financial markets. (4.74) can be tested by investigating the following restrictions:

- There is equality, respectively, between the mean and variance of the optimal current account (with asymmetry in access to the international financial market) and those of the actual value of the current account.
- CA_t^h Granger-causes future changes in net output, as defined by ΔQ_t^l, while CA_t^l does not Granger-cause ΔQ_t^h. This is to check on the implication that the future expected increase in output (ΔQ_t^h) does not impact upon the current account in the current period, while the future expected decline in output (ΔQ_t^l) generates a current account surplus in the current period.

Conclusions

This chapter has developed several variants of the present value model of the current account, ranging from models based on the assumption of a constant interest rate to a model that explicitly takes into consideration changes in the exchange rate, terms of trade and asymmetry in access to international financial markets. The theoretical contributions made in this chapter lie in using some of the features of the Nigerian economy described in Chapter 3 to produce variants of the PVMCA that capture these features. In terms of the contribution to the literature on the study of the current account, we have extended for the first time the established PVMCA to accommodate terms of trade changes. We further extended the PVMCA to accommodate possible asymmetry in access to the international financial markets. This framework can be used to analyse the current account of small industrial open economies as well as of developing countries. It is also suitable for assessing the issue of the excessiveness of current account deficits, a topic pursued later in Chapter 6.

Appendix 4.I

This Appendix demonstrates the equality of (4.36) and (4.38). To show this, we first need to derive an expression for P_t^*. To achieve this, we use the period utility function in (4.37) and the constraint that $C_t = C_{Tt} + P_t C_{NTt}$ to solve for the optimal intratemporal allocation of the total expenditure between the tradable and nontradable goods. Using the first-order condition that the marginal rate of substitution between tradable and nontradable goods should equal their relative price, we have:

$$C_{NTt} = (1-\alpha)\frac{C_t}{P_t}, \; C_{mt} = \alpha C_t \tag{4.75}$$

The optimal values of tradable and nontradable goods are substituted into the definition for C^*, which yields:

$$C_t^* = (\alpha \, C_t)^{\alpha}\left[(1-\alpha)\frac{C_t}{P_t}\right]^{1-\alpha} \tag{4.76}$$

Now use the condition that P^* is defined such that $C^* = 1$. This produces:

$$C_t^* = \left(\alpha P_t^*\right)^{\alpha}\left[(1-\alpha)\frac{P_t^*}{P_t}\right]^{1-\alpha} = 1 \tag{4.77}$$

Solving (4.77) for the consumption-based price index, P_t*, yields:

$$P_t^* = P_t^{(1-\alpha)} \left[\frac{1}{\alpha^\alpha (1-\alpha)^{(1-\alpha)}} \right] \tag{4.78}$$

Note that C_t/P_t* is the ratio of spending, measured in units of tradables, to the minimum price, in tradables, of a single unit of the consumption index. Therefore, C_t/P_t* is the index of the total real consumption of an optimising consumer.

Let:

$$C_t^* = \frac{C_t}{P_t^*}$$

Given that:

$$C_t^* = \frac{C_T + p_t C_{NTt}}{P_t^*}$$

$$P_t^* C_t^* = C_t + P_t C_{NTt} \tag{4.79}$$

This provides the justification for writing the dynamic budget constraint in (4.36) as (4.38).

Appendix 4.II[24]

Equation (4.49) was:

$$\Gamma_0 = \sum_{t=0}^{\infty} E_0 (R_t^* Q_t)$$

Equation (4.49) implies the law of motion for Γ_t:

$$\Gamma_{t+1} = (1 + r_t^*)(\Gamma_t - Q_t), \qquad \text{for } t \geq 0 \tag{4.80}$$

---

[24] This presentation follows the work of Huang and Lin (1993) closely. While their presentation focuses on fiscal policy, it is equally applicable in analyzing the current account balance.

Dividing (4.80) by Γ_t, and taking logarithms on both sides, yields:

$$\varphi_{t+1} - \varphi_t = \ln(1 + r^*_t) + \ln\left(1 - \frac{Q_t}{\Gamma_t}\right)$$

$$\approx r^* + \ln(1 - \exp(q_t - \varphi_t)) \tag{4.81}$$

where $\varphi = \log \Gamma$ and we made use of the approximation that $\log (1+r_t^*) = r_t^*$.

Next, take a first-order Taylor expansion of $\ln (1-\exp (q_t - \varphi_t))$ in (4.81) around a normal level of $(q_t - \varphi_t)$. This yields:

$$\ln(1 - \exp(q_t - \varphi_t)) \approx k + \left(1 - \frac{1}{\rho}\right)(q_t - \varphi_t) \tag{4.82}$$

Therefore, we can write (4.81) as:

$$\varphi_{t+1} - \varphi_t \approx r_t^* + k + \left(1 - \frac{1}{\rho}\right)(q_t - \varphi_t) \tag{4.83}$$

where

$$\rho = 1 - \exp(q_t - \varphi_t) = 1 - \frac{Q_t}{\Gamma_t}$$

which is a number slightly less than one and

$$k = \ln(\rho) - \left(1 - \frac{1}{\rho}\right)n(1 - \rho).$$

Note that:

$$\varphi_{t+1} - \varphi_t \approx \Delta q_{t+1} + (q_t - \varphi_t) - (q_{t+1} - \varphi_{t+1}) \tag{4.84}$$

Substituting (4.83) into (4.84) yields:

$$-(q_{t+1} - \varphi_{t+1}) + \left(\frac{1}{\rho}\right)(q_t - \varphi_t) \approx -\Delta q_{t+1} + r_t^* + k \tag{4.85}$$

Solving the above difference equation forward produces:

$$q_0 - \varphi_0 = \sum_{t=1}^{\infty} \rho^t (r^* - \Delta q_t) + \eta \qquad (4.86)$$

where $q_0 = \ln Q_0$, $\varphi_0 = \ln \Gamma_0$, $\Delta q_t = q_t - q_{t-1}$; and η is a constant.

Appendix 4.III

The derivation here is quite similar to that in Appendix 4.I. Our intention is to show that the dynamic budget constraint in (4.61) is valid. Using the first-order condition that the marginal rate of substitution between importable and nontradable goods should equal their relative price, we have:

$$C_{NTt} = \frac{(1-\alpha)}{P_{nt}} C_t; \; C_{mt} = \frac{\alpha}{P_{mt}} C_t \qquad (4.87)$$

Once we have derived the optimal choice of both importable and nontradable goods, they are substituted in the definition for C^*, which in turn yields:

$$C_t^* = \left(\frac{\alpha}{P_{mt}} C_t \right)^\alpha \left[(1-\alpha) \frac{C_t}{P_{nt}} \right]^{1-\alpha} \qquad (4.88)$$

Now we use the condition that P^* is defined such that $C^* = 1$. This gives:

$$C_t^* = \left(\frac{\alpha}{P_{mt}} P_t^* \right)^\alpha \left[(1-\alpha) \frac{P_t^*}{P_{n_t}} \right]^{1-\alpha} = 1 \qquad (4.89)$$

Solving (4.89) for the consumption-based price index, P_t^*, produces:

$$P_t^* = P_{mt}^\alpha P_{nt}^{(1-\alpha)} \left[\frac{1}{\alpha^\alpha (1-\alpha)^{(1-\alpha)}} \right] \qquad (4.90)$$

Note that C_t/P_t^* is the ratio of spending, measured in units of exportables, to the minimum price, in exportables, of a single unit of the consumption index.

Therefore, C_t/P_t^* equals the level of the total real consumption index C_t^* that an optimising consumer enjoys. Therefore:

$$C_t^* = \frac{C_t}{P_t^*}; \quad C_t = P_{mt}C_{mt} + P_{nt}C_{NTt}$$

$$C_t^* = \frac{P_m C_{mt} + P_{n_t} C_{NTt}}{P_t^*}$$

$$P_t^* C_t^* = P_{mt}C_{mt} + P_{n_t} C_{NTt} \tag{4.91}$$

This provides the justification for writing the dynamic budget constraint as (4.61).

Chapter 5

Econometric Estimation of the PVMCA for Nigeria

Introduction

This chapter presents for Nigeria our empirical investigations into the several variants of the present value model of the current account (PVMCA) developed in Chapter 4. The standard (labelled as the 'benchmark') version of the PVMCA was presented in Chapter 4 and then extended to accommodate the impact on the current account of changes in the interest rate, exchange rate and terms of trade. Also, given the political and macroeconomic instability in Nigeria during the period 1960-97, asymmetry in access to the international financial market was incorporated into one of the versions of the PVMCA developed in Chapter 4. Another variant encompassed Nigeria's Structural Adjustment Program of 1986.

This chapter estimates for the Nigerian economy the various versions of the PVMCA developed in Chapter 4. First, it reports on tests for the benchmark PVMCA. Its relatively poor performance is consistent with the mixed empirical support for it in the literature and, as argued in Chapters 3 and 4, could be attributed to its exclusion of the transmission channels though which external shocks impact on the current account. It is expected that taking the interest and exchange rates into consideration would enhance the performance of the PVMCA. Second, this chapter reports on our estimates for the version of the PVMCA that includes changes in the interest rate and exchange rate.

Third, this chapter estimates the version of the PVMCA that accommodates changes in the terms of trade. In the context of the Nigerian economy, unexpected changes in the terms of trade are the major source of external shocks. The oil price shock of the early 1970s is a good example of the sensitivity of the Nigerian economy to developments in the world oil markets. It is, therefore, important to assess whether the inclusion of changes in the terms of trade in a PVMCA that already accommodates variations in the interest rates and exchange rates would change the results obtained from not taking them into consideration.

Fourth, this chapter estimates the version of the PVMCA that allows for asymmetry in access to the international financial capital markets. Chapter 4 had noted that one of the inherent weaknesses of the benchmark PVMCA is its assumption of unrestricted access to the international financial market. We remarked in Chapter 4 that private economic agents in Nigeria and Ghana may have had no difficulty smoothing consumption in anticipation of lower income; however, in the event of higher expected income or unanticipated declines in income, they may not be able to use the international financial market to smooth consumption fully. This inability may result from a number of factors, including poor macroeconomic management, political instability and high levels of existing external debt. Asymmetrical access could also emanate from a past failure to service external obligations. Our estimates for Nigeria do establish asymmetry in access to the international financial market. Therefore, economic agents in Nigeria were not able to borrow to smooth their consumption, with a consequent decrease in their welfare level. Our interest in assessing asymmetry in access to the international financial markets also arises from the need to examine the excessiveness of current account deficits. In the event of an asymmetry in this access, deviations of actual current account balances from an optimal benchmark derived from the assumption of free capital mobility would not reveal the actual degree of external imbalances. This issue will be pursued in Chapter 6.

Further, as a follow-up to possible asymmetry in access to the international financial markets, we explore whether the oil price shocks of the early 1970s increased the Nigerian economy's access to the international financial market. It has been noted in the literature that the oil boom of the 1970s hastened the integration of the oil-exporting countries into the international financial market. This chapter uses the PVMCA framework to investigate whether this really occurred in the Nigerian case.

We also investigate whether the introduction of the Structural Adjustment Program (SAP) in Nigeria in 1986 increased the access of the economy to the international financial market. Market-oriented measures such as the market determination of the interest rates and exchange rates accompanied the introduction of the SAP. Market determination of the interest and exchange rates, coupled with sound and consistent macroeconomic management, should increase international confidence in the Nigerian economy and enhance international capital flows to the economy for the consumption-smoothing purposes. To capture these developments, the impact of the introduction of Structural Adjustment Program in 1986 on the Nigerian current account is evaluated.

Based on the time series data for Nigeria, our findings are that most of the implications of the 'final' model – incorporating interest rate movements, changes in the exchange rate and the terms of trade, and asymmetry in the international financial markets – are not rejected by the Nigerian data, so that this version of the PVMCA is a valid theoretical framework for analysing the current account. We find that this version of the PVMCA is also able to capture the evolution of the actual current account balance. However, our estimates show that Nigeria's actual current account was more volatile than the optimal one, suggesting that speculative factors were a major driving force behind capital flows. Policies of the administrative determination of the nominal exchange rate and interest rate, especially before 1986, along with macroeconomic instability, engendered speculative capital flows (including capital flights and reversals) into Nigeria. Given the condition that the current account mirrors the capital account component of the balance of payments less changes in net international reserves, the volatility in the capital flows was reflected in current account volatility.

Our empirical results also show that the introduction of the Structural Adjustment Program did not alter the relationship between the change in net output and the current account.[1] This implies that the introduction of the SAP did not lead to increased access of the Nigerian economy to the international financial market. However, our results also show that the oil price shocks of the early 1970s did bring about a significant increase in the Nigerian economy's access to the international financial markets.

This chapter has seven sections. Section 5.1 deals with the data presentation for Nigeria and specifies the sources of the data and the derivation of the variables used to conduct the empirical investigations for the PVMCA. Section 5.2 focuses on the results obtained from the empirical work on the benchmark PVMCA model (which does not consider changes in the interest rate, exchange rate and the terms of trade, and asymmetry in access to the international financial markets). Section 5.3 presents the results of the version of the PVMCA that incorporates changes in the interest rate and the exchange rate. Section 5.4 presents the results for the PVMCA incorporating also changes in the terms of trade. Section 5.5 examines the effects of incorporating asymmetry in access to the international financial markets. Section 5.6 reports our findings on the oil prices shock of 1973. Section 5.7 presents our findings related to the Structural Adjustment Program.

5.1 Data and Parameter Values for Nigeria

We use annual data from 1960 to 1997 for Nigeria. We collected data on private consumption, government consumption, investment and gross domestic product (GDP). All variables are cast in real per capita terms by dividing the nominal variables by the GDP deflator (1995=100) and total population. The National Income Accounting (NIA) data used for the analysis are from the World Bank, Social Indicators of Development database. The data on the variables used for the analysis are provided in the Data Appendix 5.II.

The actual current account series, cat, was constructed by subtracting the log of the real per capita private consumption expenditure from the log of net output.[2] The net output series qt was computed by subtracting government and

---

[1] One criterion for testing the validity of the PVMCA is to examine whether the current account Granger-causes the expected change in net output (the difference between GDP, investment and government expenditure). This is used to examine whether there has been a change in the relationship between the current account and the change in the net output both in the pre-and post-SAP periods and the pre- and post-oil prices shock periods.

[2] Bergin and Sheffrin (2000) used the same approach to arrive at the current account balance.

investment expenditures from GDP. We took the log and first difference of qt, which gives the change in net output, cneot.

Our proxy for the expected real world interest rate, rt*, was defined as the London Interbank Offer Rate (LIBOR) adjusted for the expected rate of inflation in the industrial countries. This method followed several other studies on developing economies (Nyatepe-Coo, 1993; Khan and Knight, 1983).

The available time series data on the real effective exchange rate for Nigeria covers the 1980-97 period. In order to arrive at estimates of the real effective exchange rate during 1960-97, we first compute the bilateral exchange rate between Nigeria and a specific trading partner. This is summed across six major trading partners: France, Germany, Japan, Netherlands, UK, and the USA. The weight assigned to a trading partner reflects the extent of trade flows between that partner and Nigeria. The terms of trade are defined as the relative price of imports in terms of exports. The ex-ante expected change in the exchange rate and the terms of trade are computed using a one-year autoregression. Two consumption-based interest rates were used. One of these was the consumption-based interest rate, $\hat{r}$, given by the world interest rate r* adjusted for the expected change in the exchange rate. The other was the consumption-based interest rate, $\hat{\hat{r}}$, given by the world interest rate r* adjusted for both changes in the exchange rate and the terms of trade. Given our interest in the dynamic implications of the model, the series used in the VAR processes for cneot, cat, $\hat{r}$, and $\hat{\hat{r}}$ are the deviations from their respective means.

There are three parameters that are important for implementing the PVMCA empirically: the elasticity of intertemporal substitution, γ; the share of tradable/importable goods in the total consumption expenditures, α; and the preference parameter, β. We used other studies in the literature to arrive at the estimates for these parameters. Arguments abound in the literature as to the size of the intertemporal elasticity parameter γ. Given the fact that our study allows for nontradable goods, we tend to support the position of Ostry and Reinhart (1992), that the intertemporal elasticity of substitution is different from zero. In their study, the intertemporal elasticity of substitution ranged between 0.38 and 0.50. However, for African countries, the intertemporal elasticity was 0.451 using instrument set I and 0.443 using instrument set II. The distinction between the two instrument sets was that the levels of consumption of importable and of non-traded goods were used as the instruments in the former, while their ratio was used as the instrument in the latter. The results reported in this chapter use 0.451 for the intertemporal elasticity of substitution, as there were hardly any qualitative or quantitative differences between our results for the values of 0.451 and 0.443.

The preference parameter β fell in the range from 0.96 to 0.99 for Ostry and Reinhart (1992), while our estimate is 0.97.[3] We conduct present value tests

---

[3]   In our study, $\beta = \dfrac{1}{1+\bar{r}*} = 0.97$ where $\bar{r}*$ is the average of the computed real LIBOR rate.

using 0.85^4 as the share of tradable goods in the consumption basket. The econometric techniques used are presented in Appendix 5.I.

5.2 Testing the Benchmark PVMCA[5]

For the benchmark PVMCA – when changes in the interest rate, exchange rate and asymmetry in access to the international financial market are excluded – section (4.2) of Chapter 4 derived the following equation describing the optimal current account balance.

$$ca^*_t = -[1 \ 0](\beta\Psi)(I-\beta\Psi)^{-1}\begin{bmatrix} cneo_t \\ ca_t \end{bmatrix}$$

$$= [\Phi_{\Delta cneo} \quad \Phi_{ca}]\begin{bmatrix} cneo_t \\ ca_t \end{bmatrix} \tag{5.1}$$

where Ψ is the VAR parameters, and r^* is the world interest rate.[6] To evaluate the benchmark PVMCA, we test the restriction that $[\Phi_{\Delta cneo} \ \Phi_{ca}] = [0 \ 1]$, using the delta method to calculate a $\chi 2$ statistic for the hypothesis that $k = [\Phi_{\Delta cneo} \ \Phi_{ca}] = [0 \ 1]$. Designating the difference between the actual value of k and its hypothesized value as g, and assuming that the standard errors needed for this test are given by $\left((\partial k/\partial\psi)V(\partial k/\partial\psi)'\right)^{-1}$, then $g'\left((\partial k/\partial\psi)V(\partial k/\partial\psi)'\right)^{-1}g$ will be distributed chi-squared with two degrees of freedom, where V is the variance-covariance matrix of the VAR parameters and $\partial k/\partial\psi$ is the matrix of the derivatives of the k vector with respect to these VAR parameters.

---

[4] One approach to determining the share of the nontradables in the consumption basket is to break down expenditures by categories (Kravis *et al.* 1982). Expenditures on the following categories are commonly used as the proxy for nontradables: rent, fuel, transportation and communications. Using these expenditure items, the share of nontradables in the consumption basket in Nigeria is about 15 percent.

[5] As noted in Chapter 4, the summaries of the implications of the present value model of the current account tested are: that the stationarity of the optimal current account is due to the stationarity of the change in net output; that there is equality between the optimal and actual current account; that there is equality of variances of the optimal and current accounts; and finally, that the stationarity of the optimal current account implies the stationarity of the actual current account. All these implications are applicable to the various variants of the PVMCA.

[6] The proxy used by us for this interest rate is the London Interbank Offer Rate (LIBOR).

The variables entering the VAR in equation (5.1), cneot and cat, must be stationary. The Augmented Dickey Fuller (ADF) and Phillips-Perron (PP) unit root tests presented in Table 5.1 do not include a constant and a time trend, since the variables are expressed in deviations from their means. The current account (cat) and the change in net output (cneot) are found to be stationary variables at significance levels of 5 percent. Moreover, the benchmark PVMCA through its equation (5.1) implies that the optimal current account is a stationary variable. If the benchmark PVMCA is valid, the actual current account would equal the optimal current account, so that the actual current account must also be stationary. Using the ADF and the PP unit root tests, this implication is found to be valid, as the actual current account appears to be stationary. This evidence supports the benchmark PVMCA.

The vector autoregression in $cneo_t$ and ca_t required for the evaluation of (5.1) is estimated by applying OLS to its constituent equations. The Akaike Information Criterion (AIC) and Schwarz Criterion (SC) indicated a one-lag VAR for the variables of interest, cneot and cat. The VAR parameters needed to derive the optimal current account balance in (5.1) are presented in Table 5.2a.

Tests of the restrictions implied by the benchmark PVMCA are reported in Table 5.2b. As shown in Figure 5.1, the standard model is able to predict the general direction of the movements in the current account, especially the current account deficits in the 1960s, the 1974 and 1979-80 current account surpluses arising from global increases in oil prices, the 1981-83 current account deficits and the improvements in the current account position in the last three years covered by this study. Despite this performance, the statistical test rejects the model. With one lag and two variables, the k-vector for the benchmark PVMCA is expected to be [0 1]. However, the estimated values are [-0.11 0.71]. While the coefficient on the current account at date t is statistically different from zero, it is quite different from 1 (see Table 5.2b). However, the coefficient of the change in net output, cneot, is found not to be significantly different from its theoretical value of zero. The benchmark model's current account is only 44 percent as volatile as the actual. Overall, the $\chi 2$ test strongly rejects the model, with a p-value of zero. As noted by Bergin and Sheffrin (2000), this result is typical of most previous empirical investigations in this area: while a simple graphical analysis appears to suggest that the benchmark PVMCA can explain a significant portion of the movements in the actual current account, the benchmark model rarely satisfies statistical tests.

The failure of the benchmark PVMCA in statistical tests could be attributed to the exclusion of channels through which external shocks impact upon the current account. Current account deficits in Nigeria in the mid-1980s partly reflected the governmental policy of fixing the exchange rate, which led to the appreciation of the real exchange rate. Real exchange rate appreciation lowered the cost of imported goods, which lowered the consumption-based interest rate and led to the deterioration of the current account balance. It is, therefore, not surprising that the economy had to embark on the Structural Adjustment Program of 1986.

**Table 5.1   Benchmark PVMCA (Excluding Changes in Interest Rate, Real
                Exchange rate and Terms of Trade)
                Unit Root Tests for Nigeria**

Variable (First Difference)	ADF*	PP*
Change in net output (cneo)	-5.23	-5.81
Actual Current account (ca)	-3.28	-3.40
Optimal current account (ca*)	-3.19	-3.72

* ADF indicates the Augmented Dickey-Fuller test; PP represents the
Phillip-Perron test.

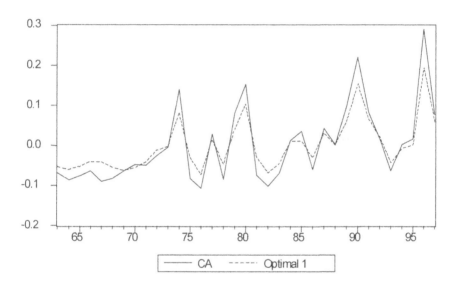

**Figure 5.1   Benchmark PVMCA (Excluding Changes in Interest Rate, Real
                Exchange Rate and Terms of Trade): Actual and Optimal
                Current Accounts for Nigeria**

Table 5.2a VAR components of the Benchmark PVMCA for Nigeria

Equation	Regressors	
	cneot-1	cat-1
cneot	0.184	-0.480
	(0.186)	(0.210)
cat	0.129	0.281
	(0.166)	(0.187)

Standard errors in parentheses.

Table 5.2b Tests of the Benchmark PVMCA for Nigeria

cneot	-0.11
	(0.13)
cat	0.71
	(0.02)

$\chi 2 = 384.59$; p-value = 0.000; var (cat*)/var (cat) = 44.32
Standard errors in parentheses.

5.3 The PVMCA Adjusted for Changes in the World Interest Rate and Real Exchange Rate

As explained in Chapters 3 and 4, the exclusion of the channels (interest rate and exchange rate) through which external shocks impact on the current account provides a possible explanation for the rejection of the stringent restrictions of the benchmark PVMCA. The results presented in Table 5.2b are broadly consistent with the findings of other studies using a present value approach that excludes changes in the interest rate and the exchange rate.

Section 4.3 of Chapter 4 presented the version of the PVMCA that incorporates changes in the interest rate and the exchange rate. Its equation for the optimal current account balance was given by:

$$hz_t = -\sum_{t=T+1}^{\infty} \beta^{t-T}(g_1 - \gamma g_2)\Psi^{t-T} z_t$$

$$(5.2)$$

The variables in (5.2) are defined as follows: $z_t = (cneo_t\ ca_t\ \hat{r}_t)'$, $g_1 = [1\ 0\ 0]$, $g_2 = [0\ 0\ 1]$, $h = [0\ 1\ 0]$ and $\hat{r}_t$ is the consumption-based interest rate that incorporates the world real interest rate and the expected change in the exchange rate. Equation (5.2) can be rewritten as:

$$ca_t{}^{**} = kz_t \qquad\qquad (5.3)$$

where $k = -(g_1 - \gamma\, g_2)\,\beta\Psi\,(1 - \beta\Psi\,)^{-1}$.

We examine the time series properties of cneot, cat, and $\hat{r}_t$, as they have to be stationary in order to enter the VAR process. We employ the value of 0.45 for the intertemporal elasticity and we use 0.85 for the share of the tradable goods. The ADF and PP unit root tests reveal the stationarity of the consumption-based interest rate. Table 5.3 reports the unit root tests. The consumption-based interest rate and the optimal current account balance are stationary variables at the 5 percent significance levels. The VAR parameters are shown in Table 5.4a and the present value tests are reported in Table 5.4b. The variant of the PVMCA model incorporating the expected change in the real exchange rate is not rejected; this result is contrary to our findings on the benchmark model that had excluded the consumption-based interest rate.

With one lag and three variables, the theoretically expected k-vector for (5.3) is [0 1 0]. However, the estimated vector is [-0.07 0.68 -0.39]. The coefficient on the change in net output is closer to its theoretical value of zero, relative to the benchmark model, while the coefficient on the current account in the PVMCA that included the consumption-based interest rate is less than that of the benchmark model. There appear to be no significant differences between the volatility of the optimal current account, when the exchange rate and interest rate movements are factored in, relative to the version of the PVMCA that excludes them, as it remains at 44 percent of the actual.[7] This indicates that, in the context of the Nigerian economy, the lower volatility of the optimal current account cannot be attributed to the exclusion of the source through which an external shock affects the current account balance.

For Nigeria, in terms of the overall performance of the intertemporal model, the $\chi 2$ test does not reject the model, with a p-value of 0.7. While the stringent restriction implied by the PVMCA is rejected in the case of the benchmark model in Section 5.3, including changes in the interest rate and the exchange rate does matter for the determination of the current account. The optimal current account when the consumption-based interest rate is introduced is shown in Figure 5.2. It closely tracks the evolution of the actual current account balance during the period 1963-97.

---

[7] This result is similar to those obtained by Bergin and Sheffrin (2000) for Canada, where there was a difference between the theoretical k-vector and the actual k, and the stringent restriction of the PVMCA was not rejected and the optimal current account is 50 percent as volatile as the actual.

While Chapter 4 had demonstrated the impact on the current account of changes in the interest rate and the exchange rate, Nigeria maintained what amounted to a fixed nominal exchange rate up to 1986. With administrative determination of the exchange rate, the Nigerian economy missed one channel that would have been used to reduce the external imbalances associated with the declining terms of trade in the first half of the 1980s. The adverse effects of nominal exchange rate overvaluation were reinforced by high domestic inflation, and growing fiscal deficits after the collapse in oil prices. This explains why the current account was excessive during 1981-1983: there was real appreciation of the exchange rate that favours excess consumption.

Table 5.3   PVMCA Incorporating the Interest Rate and the Exchange Rate Unit Root Tests for Nigeria

Variable	ADF*	PP*
Change in net output (cneo)	-5.23	-5.81
Actual Current account (ca)	-3.28	-3.40
Optimal current account (CA*)	-3.23	-4.04
Consumption-based Interest rate	-3.88	-4.17

($\gamma = 0.45$; $\alpha = 0.85$)
*   ADF indicates the Augmented Dickey-Fuller test; PP represents the Phillip-Perron test.

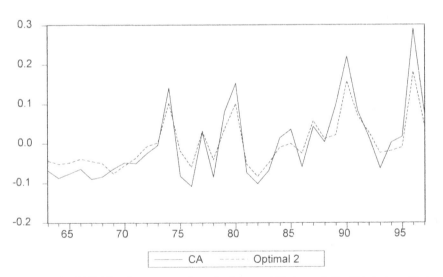

Figure 5.2   PVMCA Incorporating the Interest Rate and the Exchange Rate: Actual and Optimal Current Accounts for Nigeria

**Table 5.4a PVMCA Incorporating the Interest Rate and the Exchange Rate
VAR Components of the PVMCA for Nigeria**

Equation	Regressors		
	cneot-1	cat-1	$\hat{r}_t$
cneot	0.118	-0.465	0.718
	(0.186)	(0.203)	(0.497)
cat	0.065	0.294	0.718
	(0.164)	(0.180)	(0.440)
$\hat{r}_t$	-0.001	-0.013	0.316
	(0.066)	(0.0726)	(0.177)

Standard errors in parentheses.

**Table 5.4b PVMCA Incorporating the Interest Rate and the Exchange Rate
Tests of the PVMCA for Nigeria**

cneot	-0.07979
	(0.35024)
cat	0.68926
	(0.28534)
$\hat{r}_t$	-0.39251
	(0.50460)

$\chi 2=1.42129$; p-value=0.701; var (cat*)/var (cat)=43.8
Standard errors in parentheses.

5.4 The PVMCA Adjusted for Changes in the World Interest Rate, Real Exchange Rate and the Terms of Trade

Since changes in the terms of trade are likely to have affected the current account balance of the Nigerian economy, section 4.4 of Chapter 4 extended the benchmark PVMCA to capture the expected change in the terms of trade. With the introduction of the expected change in the terms of trade, the change in the consumption-based interest rate could come from the expected change in the world real interest rate, the real exchange rate, or/and the terms of trade.

With the introduction of changes in the terms of trade into the version of the PVMCA that already has changes in the interest rate and the exchange rate, the optimal current account balance, as demonstrated in Chapter 4, is given by:

$$hz_t = -\sum_{t=\tau+1}^{\infty} \beta^{t-\tau} (g_1 - \gamma\, g_2)\Psi^{t-\tau}\, z_t \tag{5.4}$$

where z_t= (cneot cat $\hat{r}_t$)', g1 =[1 0 0], g2=[0 0 1], and h=[0 1 0] and $\hat{r}_t$ is the consumption-based interest rate that includes the world interest rate, expected change in the exchange rate and the terms of trade. Equation (5.4) can be rewritten as:

$$ca_t{}^{**} = kz_t \tag{5.5}$$

$$k = -(g_1 - \gamma\, g_2)\beta\Psi\, (I - \beta\Psi)^{-1}$$

The variables cneot, cat, and $\hat{r}_t$ entering the VAR are examined for their degrees of integration. We use 0.45 as the value for the intertemporal elasticity and 0.85 for the share of tradables. The unit root tests show that the variables of interest are integrated of order zero. Table 5.5 reports the unit root tests. The consumption-based interest rate and the optimal current account balance are found to be stationary at the 5 percent significance level. The stationarity of the optimal current account balance is evidence in favour of the PVMCA. The VAR parameters are shown in Table 5.6a and the present value tests are reported in Table 5.6b.

The inclusion of changes in the terms of trade does not appear to improve the fit of the PVMCA provided that it had already incorporated the interest rate and the exchange rate. However, it outperforms the benchmark PVMCA, which does not incorporate the transmission mechanisms through which an external source can impact on the current account. The coefficient on the current account at date t was 0.680, instead of the theoretical value of 1. This is less than 0.69, when the changes in the interest rate and exchange rate are considered. The coefficient on the change in net output, cneot, is -0.12, which is different from its theoretical value of 0. It is also different from -0.08, when the terms of trade were not considered. The coefficient of the consumption-based interest rate when the terms of trade were taken into consideration was -0.02, whereas it was 0.39 when they were not taken into consideration.

Moreover, the volatility of the optimal current account is 43 percent of that of the actual current account. This is close to the value obtained when changes in the terms of trade are excluded. Lastly, the $\chi 2$ test does not reject the version of the PVMCA that incorporates the interest rate, the real exchange rate and the terms of trade.

Recognizing that an unexpected temporary deterioration in the terms of trade produces an income effect, the intertemporal and intratemporal effects can explain the above results. Given consumption smoothing, the income effect of an increase in the relative price of importables would produce current account deterioration. The intratemporal effect would encourage postponing the consumption of tradables in the current period. The fall in the terms of trade makes nontradables cheaper, leading to increased demand for the nontradables, with consequent real exchange rate appreciation. Thus, the overall impact of a temporary but unanticipated change in the terms of trade depends on the income, intratemporal and intertemporal effects. The inclusion of the change in the terms of trade and the real exchange rate in the definition of the consumption-based interest implies that the terms of trade capture the intertemporal effects and the real exchange rate captures the intratemporal effect. The similarity in the empirical findings between the PVMCA that accommodates the real exchange rate and the one that does not, suggests that the intratemporal effect of a shock may be more important in the Nigerian context than its intertemporal effect.

5.5 Asymmetry in the Access to the International Financial Market

It was postulated in Chapter 4 that private agents in Nigeria and Ghana might not have full or complete access to the international financial markets. This could be a result of political instability, macroeconomic instability or/and a high level of existing external obligations. The existence of these factors could weaken the ability of economic agents to meet existing and new external obligations that may fall due, and reduce the willingness of lenders to lend to them.

Table 5.5   **PVMCA Incorporating the Interest Rate, Exchange Rate and the Terms of Trade**
            Unit Root Tests for Nigeria

Variable	ADF*	PP*
Change in net output (cneo)	-5.23	-5.81
Actual Current account (ca)	-3.28	-3.40
Optimal current account	3.33	-3.88
Consumption-based Interest rate	4.64	-5.66

$\gamma=0.45$; $\alpha=0.5$
* ADF indicates the Augmented Dickey-Fuller test; PP represents the Phillip-Perron test.

In order to test this proposition, Chapter 4 extended the PVMCA that already has changes in the interest rate and exchange rate to reflect this financial market imperfection. Taking this factor into consideration produces a path of the current account balance that is different from the one under the assumption of unrestricted access to the international financial market. Despite the fact that the economy may be solvent, the prevalence of factors that weaken the ability of

:9: 9 9 9 9 9:9 99999

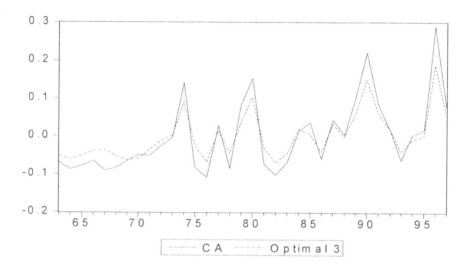

Figure 5.3   PVMCA Incorporating the Interest Rate, Exchange Rate and the Terms of Trade: Actual and Optimal Current Accounts for Nigeria

where $z_t = (cneo^h_t \; cneo^l_t \; ca^h_t \; ca^l_t \; \hat{r}_t \;)'$, $g_1 = [1\ 1\ 0\ 0\ 0]$, $g_2 = [0\ 0\ 0\ 0\ 1]$, and $h = [0\ 0\ 1\ 1\ 0]$; ca^h_t (ca^l_t) equals ca_t when ca_t is positive (negative) and ca^h_t (ca^l_t) is zero; and $cneo^h_t$ ($cneo^l_t$) equals $cneo_t$ when $cneo_t$ is positive (negative) and $cneo^h_t$ ($cneo^l_t$) is zero. Rewrite (5.6) as:

$$ca_t^{****} = kz_t \tag{5.7}$$

where $k = -(g_1 - \gamma g_2)\beta\Psi(I - \beta\Psi)^{-1}$.

    Our empirical estimates for Nigeria show that asymmetry in access to the international financial markets is not rejected, as indicated by a p-value of 0.6. This implies that the imposition of asymmetry in access to the international financial market is a valid restriction. The estimated k vector is [0.14 -0.18 0.72 0.49 -0.46], which is quite different from the theoretically expected k vector [0 0 1 1 0].

    To further investigate this, a simple Granger-causality test was conducted to examine if the expectations of higher output led to current account deficits and if the expectations of lower output resulted in current account surpluses. According to this test, the current account is said to cause the change in net output if the change in net output is significantly better predicted using the past values of both the change in net output and the current account balance than using only the past values of the change in net output. A finding that the expectation of an increase in net output do not Granger-cause the current account deficit, and that expectations of a decrease in net output do Granger-cause the current account surplus, would be evidence in favour of restricted access to the international financial market. The null of no Granger-causality between ca^l_t (which equals ca_t when ca_t is negative and zero otherwise – i.e., in the case of current account deficit) and $cneo^h_t$ (which equals $cneo_t$, when $cneo_t$ is positive and zero otherwise, i.e., when an increase in net output is expected) is not rejected at the 5 percent level for Nigeria: it has an F-value of 0.13 and a p-value of 0.72. This can be interpreted to mean that, for the Nigerian economy, the expectation of higher output does not necessarily result in a current account deficit in the current period. However, the null that ca^h_t (which equals ca_t when ca_t is positive and zero otherwise – current account surplus) does not Granger-cause $cneo^l_t$ (which equals $cneo_t$, when $cneo_t$ is positive and zero otherwise, i.e., when a fall in net output is expected) is rejected: the F-value is 4.09 and the associated p-value is 0.03.

The results above indicate that asymmetry in access to the international financial market is important for Nigeria's current account. This asymmetry is likely to have occurred due to a lack of confidence in the Nigerian economy because of the macroeconomic and political situation in the country. In the context of complete financial markets, one can expect the market to base the risk-premium on the perceived risks, thereby charging appropriately higher interest rates. However, such an interest rate becomes sufficiently high to dissuade private economic agents from borrowing in the organized capital markets. Further, there is usually a rationing element in financial markets due to the presence of adverse selection and moral hazard. Such rationing becomes more stringent in periods of macroeconomic and political instability, especially when there is a significant likelihood of exchange rate depreciation. Hence, stable macroeconomic and political conditions matter for capital inflows into the economy.

The graphical representations of both the actual and optimal current accounts (with asymmetry in access) are presented in Figure 5.4.

5.6 The PVMCA and Nigeria's Structural Adjustment Program

To accommodate the introduction of the Structural Adjustment Program (SAP) in Nigeria in 1986, both the current account and the change in net output were partitioned into two groups: before and after the introduction of the adjustment program in 1986.[8] This produces two current accounts and two changes in net output, which gives four restrictions; the associated k-vector is [0 0 1 1 0].

---

[8] Note that this procedure is based on the use of a simple, one-step dummy variable to separate the pre- and post-1986 periods. Such a procedure is common in econometric studies to deal with data breaks. However, in all likelihood, the post-SAP effects would have been gradual and taken several years to complete, so that our results here need to be treated with caution.

However, our estimate of the k coefficient vector for Nigeria is (-0.20, -0.165, 0.511 1.086 -0.3824). The $\chi 2$ test rejects the model, with a p-value of 0.00.

We also used Granger-causality to examine the relationship before and after the introduction of the SAP between the current account and the change in the net output. The hypothesis that the current account does not Granger-cause the change in the net output in the pre-SAP period is rejected for Nigeria at the 0.004 significance level; the same hypothesis for the post-SAP era is rejected at the 0.00 significance level. This tends to show that the introduction of the SAP does not seem to have had significant impact on the ability of the economic agents in Nigeria to smooth consumption in response to temporary shocks.[9]

Figure 5.5 graphs Nigeria's actual and optimal current account balances when the introduction of the Structural Adjustment is taken into consideration.

5.7 The Present Value Tests and the Oil Price Shock

To reflect the impact of the 1973 oil shock on the current account determination, both the current account and the change in net output were divided into two categories: before and after the oil price shock in 1973. This produces two current accounts and two changes in net output, and introduces four restrictions: the coefficients on the two changes in net outputs are expected to be zero and the two current accounts have the expected value of 1. However, our estimate of the k coefficient vector for Nigeria is (-0.11, -0.67, 0.47 0.63 -0.79). The restrictions implied by introducing the price shock into our model were not rejected, as indicated by a p-value of 0.45.

Granger-causality was used to examine for Nigeria the relationship between the current account and the change in net output before and after the oil price shock of 1973. For Nigeria, with a p-value of 0.58, the F test rejects the hypothesis that the current account Granger-caused the change in net output in the pre-1973 period. However, the same hypothesis for the post-1973 period was not rejected by the F-test, which has a p-value of 0.02. This is consistent with the intuitive observation that the increase in oil prices in 1973 opened the Nigerian economy to the international financial market. But, after the drop in oil prices, the country was unable to maintain consumption at a sustainable level and resorted to short-term borrowing. It is, therefore, not surprising that we see a change in the relationship between the change in net output and the current account after the oil price shock of 1973.

Figure 5.6 graphs the actual and optimal current account balances for Nigeria when the oil price shock of 1973 is taken into account.

---

[9] This is not an attempt to evaluate the impact of the SAP on the Nigerian economy. The basic question is whether the introduction of this program led to an increase in access to the international capital markets or not.

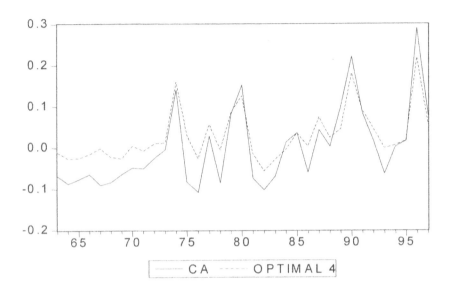

Figure 5.4 PVMCA Incorporating the Interest Rate and Exchange Rate, and Asymmetry in Capital Flows: Actual and Optimal Current Account Balances for Nigeria

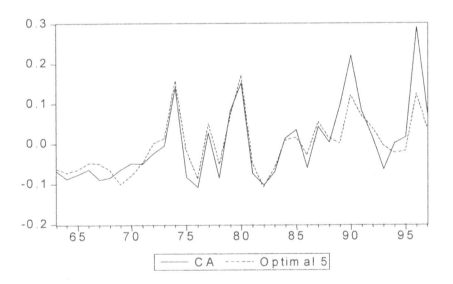

Figure 5.5 PVMCA Incorporating the Interest rate and Exchange Rate: Actual and Optimal Current Accounts for Nigeria

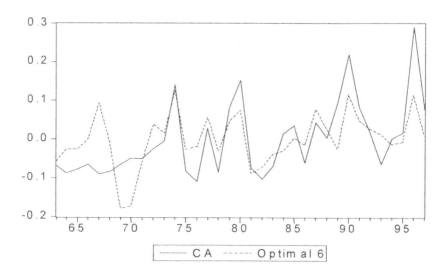

Figure 5.6 PVMCA Incorporating the Interest Rate and Exchange Rate, and Oil Price Shocks: Actual and Optimal Current Accounts for Nigeria

Conclusions

The benchmark version of the PVMCA, presented in Chapter 4, allows for domestic shocks arising from government and investment expenditures and output, without accommodating the channels through which external shocks would impact upon the current account. Our extension of the PVMCA in Chapter 4 to accommodate the real exchange rate meant taking into consideration the transmission mechanism through which external shocks impact on the current account. Further, by explicitly taking into consideration the impact of changes in the terms of trade on the current account, we factored in another significant determinant of the current account balance. Chapter 4 derived the relevant versions of the PVMCA and this chapter tested them.

For Nigeria, the benchmark PVMCA, which excluded changes in the interest rate, terms of trade and real exchange rate, was statistically rejected. But the version of the PVMCA that accommodates changes in the interest rate and the real exchange rate was not rejected. However, the volatility of the optimal current account was very similar between these two versions of the PVMCA.

Introducing the terms of trade into the PVMCA for Nigeria did not improve its fit. One possible explanation for this finding could be that the intratemporal effect of changes in the terms of trade is more important than the intertemporal effect. Hence, for analysing the current account from an intertemporal perspective, the channels through which external shock impact on the current account must be taken into consideration.

Establishing that changes in the terms of trade have intratemporal and intertemporal effects is important for understanding the behaviour of economic agents in responding to external shocks, such as a deterioration in the terms of trade. These effects need to be taken into account by the government in formulating its policies.

Support for the intertemporal model of the current account implies that the policy pursued must take into account the source of the deficits. For example, in the PVMCA, an unexpected temporary increase in government expenditures is associated with a decrease in current income relative to permanent income. Under the consumption-smoothing hypothesis, current saving decreases, and with a constant investment level, the current account position deteriorates. This current account deficit represents a rational response on the part of economic agents and there is no need for policy measures to address the imbalance.

The hypothesis of asymmetry in access to the international financial market was tested for Nigeria in this chapter and was not rejected. This was confirmed by the Granger-causality test, which indicated that the expectations of higher output were accompanied by current account surpluses, while the expectations of lower output did not necessarily lead to current account deficits.

For Nigeria, irrespective of the theoretical variant of the PVMCA used for the empirical investigation, the actual current account proved to be more volatile than the optimal one, which implies that the capital movements were sensitive to speculative factors. Capital flows are said to be excessive if they are driven by speculative forces rather than by economic fundamentals. Given asymmetry, which this chapter established, capital outflows will have excess volatility during times of macroeconomic and political instability. Noting that the current account can be defined as the sum of the capital account plus the change in net international reserves, private capital flows that are not offset by changes in reserves must be reflected in the current account. Hence, the volatility of the capital flows results in the excessive volatility of the current account.

For Nigeria, our tests of the PVMCA show that the consumption driven external imbalances in the face of declining net output in the mid-1980s resulted in unsustainable consumption levels, which led to the introduction of the Structural Adjustment Program in 1986. This suggests that the government should use an oil stabilization arrangement under which the government saves much of any temporary increases in oil revenue.

Finally, our analysis has shown that not all current account deficits are due to overvaluation of the exchange rate (as the elasticities approach to the current account suggests) or unsustainable aggregate expenditures (as the absorption approach suggests). They could, instead, be due to consumption smoothing in the face of temporary and unanticipated shocks, as in the PVMCA. In this intertemporal analysis, since economic agents smooth consumption, a temporary reduction in the domestic output (for example, a temporary negative productivity shock) will be accompanied by a current account deficit. The intertemporal approach thus adds another perspective on the determinants of the current account balance. The important policy question is: which current account imbalances are justified and which ones are not? This is examined in Chapter 6.

Appendix 5.1

Econometric Techniques and Issues

This section presents a succinct description of the econometric techniques used by us for testing the various versions of the PVMCA. In particular, we discuss the following techniques: Unit Roots Tests, Vector Autoregression, Granger Causality tests, and statistical inference.

Unit Roots Tests

The standard inference procedures depend significantly on the assumption of stationary time series. In the event that this assumption is violated, the inference drawn from the estimated parameters is invalid (Dolado *et al.*, 1990). Recognition of this has culminated in the development of various procedures for testing the presence of unit roots in time series data. In order to test for the presence of unit roots, and hence the degrees of integration of these variables, two unit root tests are used: the Augmented Dickey-Fuller (ADF) unit-root test (see Said and Dickey, 1984) and the Phillips-Perron unit-root test (see Phillips and Perron, 1988). These approaches have low power against plausible trend-stationary alternatives. This weakness should be kept in mind when interpreting the results obtained from their applications. To determine whether the relevant time series are stationary, we ran an Augmented Dickey-Fuller (ADF) test for a unit root. This involves the regression of the first difference of each variable against each lagged value, and lagged difference terms. The critical values developed by McKinnon are then used to determine the significance of the coefficients on the lagged values of the variable. If the coefficients of the lagged variable are not significantly different from 0, the null hypothesis implying the existence of a unit root cannot be rejected.

The ADF test makes a parametric correction for higher order correlation by assuming that the relevant time series follows an AR(ρ) process and therefore controls for higher-order correlation by adding lagged difference terms of the dependent variable to the regression equation. To complement the results obtained from the use of the ADF test, we employ the Phillips and Perron (1988) unit root test. Phillips and Perron proposed a nonparametric method for controlling for higher-order serial correlation in a series. The correction is nonparametric because it uses an estimate of the spectrum of the residual at frequency zero that is robust to heteroscedasticity and autocorrelation of unknown form.

Vector Autoregression

The vector autoregression technique is commonly used to explore relationships among systems of interrelated time series. The VAR approach models every endogenous variable in the system as a function of the lagged values of all of the endogenous variables in the system. Since only the lagged values of the endogenous variables appear on the right-hand side of each equation, there is no issue of simultaneity, and ordinary least square (OLS) is the appropriate estimation technique. The OLS is used in the estimation of the basic model of current account determination and the VAR is used in the empirical implementation of the PVMCA.

Granger Causality

The Granger (1969) approach to the question of whether x causes y is to see how much of the current y can be explained by past values of y and then to see whether adding lagged values of x can improve the explanation; y is said to be Granger-caused by x if x helps in the prediction of y, or equivalently if the coefficients on the lagged x's are statistically significant.

There are three principal issues concerning our use of the Granger-causality test. First, we want to explore the proposition that in the face of asymmetry in the access to the international financial market, the expected decrease in the net output will result in an increase in the current account balance, while the expectations of higher output may not necessarily result in a current account deficit in the current period. Second, we aim to investigate whether there is any significant difference between the change in net output before and after the oil prices shock of 1973. Third, we are interested in exploring the relationship between the change in net output before and after the introduction of the Structural Adjustment Program.

Statistical Inference

Most of the statistical inferences depend on the normality of the error terms in the regression equation. We use the Jarque-Berra (J-B) statistic to test for the assumption of normality of residual. Under the null hypothesis of a normal distribution, the J-B statistic is distributed as a χ^2 with 2 degrees of freedom. The reported probability is the probability that a J-B statistic exceeds (in absolute value) the observed value under the null hypothesis of a normal distribution. Under the null, the hypothesis of normality in the error terms is rejected if the computed statistic is less than the critical value. The Lagrange Multiplier (LM) test, which is applicable to any form of autocorrelation and is independent of the influence of lagged dependent variables, is also reported. The LM statistic is distributed as a χ^2 with degrees of freedom equal to the number of lagged error terms in the regression (i.e., the form of autocorrelation). The null hypothesis of the LM test is that there is no serial correlation up to lag order p. In addition, we report the

ARCH statistic, which tests for the existence of autoregressive conditional heteroscedasticity in the residuals. As noted by Engle (1982), this type of heteroscedasticity is common in time series data. The ARCH statistic is distributed as a $\chi 2$, as in the LM test. It should, however, be noted that the J-B, LM and the ARCH statistics are not exact. Their distributions are known for large sample sizes and care should be taken in using them when the sample size is small.

Standard errors needed to test the restrictions of the PVMCA are calculated numerically as $(\partial k/\partial \psi)/V(\partial k/\partial \psi)'$, where V is the variance-covariance matrix of the underlying parameters in the VAR, and $(\partial k/\partial \psi)$ is the matrix of derivatives of the k vector with respect to these underlying parameters.[10]

---

[10] The k-vector is the expected coefficients on the change in net output, current account and consumption-based interest rate. Paul Bergin (UCLA) and Paul Cashin (IMF) provided Gauss codes used for the estimation.

Data Appendix 5.II

	Per Cap. Real GDP in Naira	Per Cap. Priv. Cons in Naira	Per Capita Invest. in Naira	Per Capita Gov. Exp. in Naira	World Int. Rate	Terms of Trade	Real Eff. Exch. Rate
1960	1247	1128	139.42	76.16	na	na	75.96
1961	1219	1086	142.99	75.19	na	96.09	77.94
1962	1236	1097	130.30	74.18	na	100.84	79.36
1963	1308	1148	146.24	75.49	0.93	97.15	74.93
1964	1337	1158	177.94	83.92	1.72	118.29	73.55
1965	1365	1131	210.23	93.55	1.85	120.24	74.03
1966	1273	1068	176.84	81.34	2.25	122.81	78.33
1967	1044	889	142.68	78.15	2.24	123.50	73.53
1968	1003	850	124.23	87.85	2.70	121.77	71.84
1969	1213	975	147.88	138.81	7.65	125.63	75.66
1970	1475	1177	218.75	121.31	3.64	132.83	81.26
1971	1640	1244	307.07	134.22	1.68	102.45	87.89
1972	1649	1153	347.71	161.65	0.81	104.17	88.67
1973	1690	1127	378.73	173.99	2.01	86.19	81.59
1974	1826	1164	309.90	157.98	-1.52	37.17	86.77
1975	1681	1120	424.23	211.75	-2.66	39.35	104.80
1976	1781	1114	560.57	207.95	-2.05	36.25	124.80
1977	1833	1024	519.34	246.48	-2.14	35.23	125.74
1978	1676	1010	461.60	275.41	1.97	41.48	135.53
1979	1736	1012	383.38	240.53	3.39	40.86	140.07
1980	1754	990	372.79	212.14	2.87	30.79	150.29
1981	1476	1002	343.83	190.14	7.01	44.03	162.70
1982	1427	997	285.53	229.39	6.35	55.36	161.76
1983	1309	935	193.08	232.22	4.63	59.92	187.63
1984	1208	857	115.10	213.06	6.21	35.88	254.79
1985	1285	949	115.31	174.00	4.14	42.45	230.63
1986	1279	947	192.28	183.00	3.78	87.13	103.81
1987	1233	850	197.13	137.31	3.84	83.74	44.87
1988	1316	893	237.14	172.17	4.41	99.81	58.12
1989	1371	882	243.18	143.17	4.69	87.13	53.92
1990	1442	801	212.58	217.79	3.21	68.72	47.23
1991	1468	859	344.10	178.72	1.63	82.00	42.11
1992	1468	852	320.23	270.03	0.35	85.30	32.86
1993	1457	908	339.52	255.16	0.22	92.50	40.95
1994	1417	922	278.25	202.08	2.30	97.86	62.11
1995	1410	997	227.05	156.43	3.20	100.00	100.00

	Per Cap. Real GDP in Naira	Per Cap. Priv. Cons in Naira	Per Capita Invest. in Naira	Per Capita Gov. Exp. in Naira	World Int. Rate	Terms of Trade	Real Eff. Exch. Rate
1996	1429	836	182.42	114.80	2.91	79.17	129.33
1997	1440	1002	220.87	122.68	5.86	76.31	143.68

Sources: World Bank: Social Indicators Database.
IMF: International Financial Statistics database.

Chapter 6

The Traditional Models of the Current Account and External Imbalances Sustainability in Nigeria

Introduction

The main objective of this chapter is to assess the external position of the Nigerian economy during the period covered by this book (1960-97). Three important and highly connected questions are regularly asked in assessing the severity of external imbalances: Are the current account imbalances sustainable? Is the debtor country solvent? Are the current account imbalances excessive?[1] Given the historical experience of recurring current account deficits and the broad increase in debt to GDP ratio, answers to these questions are important in the context of the Nigerian economy.

In respect to sustainability, one approach that has been used in the literature, which is adopted in this chapter,[2] is to consider a wide array of macroeconomic and structural factors to assess the possibility that a country is likely to experience external crisis given the continuation of the current policy mix. Justifications for using macroeconomic and structural variables to assess the external position of an economy have both intratemporal and intertemporal underpinnings. Hence, both the traditional approaches (static analyses) and the intertemporal approaches are relevant.

As remarked by Corsetti *et al.* (1998), rather than providing a unifying theoretical framework for the study of external imbalance, the approach based on the notion of sustainability primarily focuses on the empirical analysis of macroeconomic performance during crisis episodes. In light of this, this chapter uses macroeconomic and structural indicators that reflect the position of various theories of current determination, especially the traditional approach and the PVMCA to determine the sustainability of the Nigerian external imbalances during the periods preceding the external crisis of 1986. The use of additional macroeconomic and structural indicators in this chapter equally point to the

---

[1]   See Chapter 2 for the discussion of the following concepts: sustainability, solvency and excessiveness.

[2]   A number of macroeconomic indicators were used to assess the sustainability of the Nigerian external imbalances, especially in the early to mid 1980s. This chapter focuses on variables that are not included in the analysis in Chapter 2.

unsustainability of the Nigerian current account deficits in the period preceding the 1986 external crisis.

Answering the question of whether the economy is solvent or not requires a forward-looking analysis. Since traditional models are based on a static framework, they cannot be used to answer this question. However, the PVMCA meets this requirement, as it recognizes the constraint that, over an infinite horizon, the present discounted value of income must equal consumption for a given economy. This chapter deals with the solvency issue by using an empirical approach that determines a current account balance that ensures that external debt to GDP ratio is constant over time. A constant external debt to GDP ratio is considered to be a signal that the economy is in a position to service its external obligation. In this regard, this chapter determines the level of the current account balance (exclusive of interest payments) that ensures that the external debt to GDP ratio is non-increasing over time. The current account balance that ensures the constancy of external debt to GDP is then compared with the actual current account balance. The difference between the two gives some indication as to the extent of the resource gap in the economy and whether the external position is sustainable or not. A non-increasing external debt GDP ratio condition is used to assess the sustainability of the Nigerian external position in the 1980s; the results reveal significant resource gaps in the year preceding the occurrence of the external crisis in 1986.

To determine whether a given current account balance is excessive, we need a model that yields a prediction of the optimal current account balance in the face of optimal capital flows. The PVMCA is an intertemporal approach that can be used to construct this optimal current account, but the traditional model cannot be used for this purpose, since it is not designed to deal with this interesting issue. Therefore, this chapter assesses the excessiveness of the Nigerian current account deficits during the period 1960-97. Using the PVMCA, we establish that the Nigerian current account deficits were excessive in the period preceding the external crisis of 1986. It was therefore not a surprise that the country experienced an external crisis in 1986.

This chapter appears to be the first in-depth country analysis for any sub-Saharan African country using the concepts of sustainability and excessiveness. Previous studies did this for industrial and emerging economies. In addition, it is established that capital outflows from Nigeria are important variables for assessing the external position of the Nigerian economy.

Before we investigate the external position of the Nigerian economy, the next three sections of this chapter are devoted to the traditional approaches to modelling the current account (section 6.3), the econometric specification of the determinants of the current account based on these traditional models and other variables (section 6.4) and empirical results (section 6.4). This, we believe, will ensure ease of exposition as to why we would choose one model above another in answering each of the three questions raised above.

Section 6.4 reveals that changes in the world real interest rate, exchange rate, terms of trade and fiscal balance are important determinants of the current account. This section has its unique contributions. First, in terms of data coverage, this section encompasses a longer data span than any other study on current account determination in Nigeria. Second, it examines the time series properties of the relevant variables for stationarity, before proceeding to further estimation.

Section 6.5 compares the PVMCA and the traditional models of the current account. The basic message arising from this comparison is that the fact that static regression supports the position of the traditional models of the current account does not validate these models. Intertemporal models can be used to characterize the results as well. Therefore, we identify and discuss some criteria that can be used to choose between the PVMCA and the traditional approaches. Section 6.6 presents the results from using additional structural and macroeconomic indicators to assess the sustainability of the Nigerian current account balance before the year 1986. Empirical implementation of the solvency condition is presented in section 6.7. Section 6.8 presents the results of using the PVMCA to determine the excessiveness of the Nigerian current account deficits. Section 6.9 concludes the chapter.

6.1 The Traditional Models of the Current Account[3]

This section presents traditional theories of current account determination to motivate the choice of explanatory variables used to establish quantitative relationships between the current account and its major determinants in section 6.4. The three traditional approaches to current account modelling are the elasticities, absorption and monetary approaches. These models have the implications that external imbalances are driven by domestic policy and can be corrected by an appropriate combination of exchange rate and monetary policies. Each of these approaches is discussed in turn, with special attention to their derivations and weaknesses.

The Elasticities Approach

The elasticities approach focuses on the trade balance component of the current account, and accordingly emphasizes relative international prices as its central determinant. It deals with the impact of devaluation on the trade balance. Within this context, a devaluation policy improves the trade balance of the country concerned if the sum of the elasticities of imports and exports is greater than one. This is the so-called Marshall-Lerner condition.

A policy of exchange rate devaluation improves the trade balance by increasing foreigners' demand for exports of goods and services of the home economy, and by discouraging imports of foreign goods and services. The inclusion of relative prices in the empirical specification of the determinants of the current account in equation (6.12) is based on the following equations:

---

[3] See, for example, Mwau and Handa (1995), Hooper and Marquez (1995) for further details on the traditional approaches to modelling the current account.

$$EX_t = EX_t(R_t, Y_{ft})$$ (6.1)

$$IM_t = IM_t(R_t)$$ (6.2)

$$R_t = e_t \cdot \frac{P_{ft}}{P_{dt}}$$ (6.3)

$$TB_t = EX_t(R_t, Y_{ft}) - R_t \cdot IM_t(R_t)$$ (6.4)

where EX is exports, IM is imports, R is the real exchange rate, TB is the trade balance expressed in terms of domestic goods, Y_f is the foreign income, P_f represents the foreign country price index, P_d is the home country price index, e is the nominal exchange rate defined as the domestic price of a unit of foreign currency.

Equation (6.1) gives the demand function for exports, while equation (6.2) gives that of imports. Equation (6.3) defines the real exchange rate. Equation (6.4) defines the trade balance as the difference between exports and imports. From (6.4), three variables determine the current account balance, the nominal exchange rate, the foreign price index relative to that of the home country and the foreign income. As the current account balance contains both the trade balance and interest payments on outstanding foreign liabilities, equation (6.4) can be re-written as:

$$TB_t = EX_t(R_t, Y_{f_t}) - R_t \cdot IM_t(R_t) + r_t^* B_{t-1}$$ (6.5)

where r* is the real world interest rate and B is the outstanding stock of foreign liabilities. Equation (6.5) captures the basic insight of the elasticity approach by including real exchange rate among the principal determinants of the current account.

The elasticity approach has a number of inherent weaknesses. First, it does not consider the whole current account, but only a portion of it. Second, while the elasticity approach has the impact of devaluation on the current account as its main theme, no attempt is made to explicitly incorporate the non-tradable goods in order to arrive at the real exchange rate. Third, the central implication of the elasticity approach – that a nominal devaluation equals real devaluation requires appropriate fiscal and monetary policies that will prevent devaluation from leading to increase in domestic prices. In the event that a devaluation policy was accompanied by an expansionary fiscal policy and monetary accommodation of fiscal policies, the domestic price level increase and the initial nominal devaluation would have little or no impact on the real exchange rate and consequently no effect on the trade balance.

The Absorption Approach

While the elasticity approach deals with the responses of imports and exports to a reduction in the value of a country's currency, the absorption approach examines the income effects of the same policy. Currency devaluation is expected to generate expenditure-switching and expenditure-reducing effects. These two effects are expected to produce an improvement in the trade balance (Meade, 1951; Alexander, 1952).

The absorption approach to the current account seeks to remove external imbalance through adjustments in the absorption of goods and services. In equilibrium in the commodity market, domestic output or income (Y) equals expenditure, which consists of the private consumption (C), government consumption (G), investment (I), exports (EX) and imports (IM).

$$Y = C + I + G + EX - IM \qquad (6.6)$$

Combining (C+I+G) expenditure term into a single term, A, we have domestic absorption (i.e., total domestic expenditure) and X-M terms into TB (trade balance), we have:

$$Y = A + TB \qquad (6.7)$$

Equation (6.7) can be re-expressed as:

$$TB = Y - A = Y - C - G - I \qquad (6.8)$$

Based on (6.8), the absorption approach identifies reductions in the level of absorption as the principal means of improving the current account balance in the short-run. The policy instrument identified to achieve this is the exchange rate. Exchange rate devaluation through the substitution effects (expenditure switching) encourages a reduction in imports as economic agents switch from consuming foreign goods to domestic goods. The income effects (expenditure reducing) also enhance a reduction in consumption, leading to an improvement in the current account balance.

The absorption approach focuses on the income effects of devaluation without an analysis of the price effects of the same policy, as postulated by the elasticity approach. Moreover, it lacks an intertemporal context by tying current consumption to current income. This weakness is also applicable to the elasticities approach.

The Monetary Approach

The main argument of the monetary approach is that the balance of payments determination is essentially a monetary phenomenon, so that disequilibrium in the money market will be associated with a balance of payments disequilibrium (i.e., a deficit or surplus). This approach has the testable implication that a government that engages in continuous money supply expansion experiences a reduction in the level of official reserves (Polak, 1957; Frankel and Johnson, 1976; IMF, 1977). Consequently, improvements in the levels of international reserves of a monetary authority require a contractionary monetary policy.

The simplest version of the monetary approach to the balance of payments can be derived from the following identities:[4]

$$M_t = NFA_t + NDA_t \qquad (6.9)$$

where M is the stock of money, NFA is net foreign assets and NDA is net domestic assets of the domestic financial system. Approximating (6.9) by its growth form, we have:

$$\frac{\Delta NFA_t}{NFA_{t-1}} = \frac{\Delta M_t}{M_{t-1}} - \frac{\Delta NDA_t}{NDA_{t-1}} \qquad (6.10)$$

The relationship between the current and capital accounts of the balance of payments is given by:

$$NFA_t = CA_t + KA_t \qquad (6.11)$$

where CA is the current account and KA is the capital account of the balance of payments.

We assume an open economy with a fixed exchange rate regime. Equation (6.9) represents the basic identity in the money market. The stock of money is defined as the net foreign assets plus the net domestic assets. Equation (6.10) specifies that the change in net foreign assets equals the difference between the change in the money stock (or the flow demand for money) and the domestic component of money supply (i.e., net domestic assets). Equation (6.11) captures the balance of payments identity, that the change in the net foreign assets equals the sum of the current and the capital accounts.

Equation (6.10) is the fundamental equation of the monetary approach to the balance of payment. It postulates that reserves will decrease (increase) if the domestic money supply growth (credit creation) exceeds (is below) domestic money demand. In addition, from equation (6.11), a balance of payments deficit (surplus) will be reflected in a decline (increase) in net international reserves. This implies that an increase in credit creation, with a constant demand for credit, will result in a decline in reserves, and hence a deterioration of the balance of payments.

---

[4] See Polak (2001) for this definition of the money stock.

The main insight from the monetary approach is that disequilibrium in the money market has a bearing on current account determination. Despite its usefulness in identifying monetary expansion as the source of internal and external disequilibria, the monetary approach fails to account for real factors such as the real exchange rate and the terms of trade that are important for the determination of net exports and the current account in Nigeria. Moreover, this approach is more applicable to an economy with fixed exchange rates, as its implications may not hold when the market determines the exchange rate. It is more or less a model of the balance of payments adjustment and not principally that of a current account determination.

6.2 Empirical Specification of the Traditional Approaches to Modelling the Current Account

Based on equation (6.5) and the insights from the monetary approach in (6.10) and (6.11), a quantitative relationship between the current account balance and its different determinants is given by (6.12). This specification includes additional variables apart from those identified by the traditional models. The current account balance for Nigeria is specified for econometric estimation as:

$$cagdp = f(R, \ r^*, y_f, fdgdp \ .tot \ ) \tag{6.12}$$

where cagdp is the current account balance expressed as a percentage of *GDP*, R is the real effective exchange, r^* is the world real interest rate, fdgdp stands for the domestic budget balance as a ratio of GDP, y_f is the real output in the industrial countries and tot is the terms of trade. The specification in (6.12) is along the lines of similar studies for small open economies (Khan and Knight, 1983; Pastor, 1989).

Within the traditional models of current account determination, we expect an improvement in the terms of trade or an increase in the growth rates of industrial countries to bring about an improvement in the current account. However, a rise in the foreign real interest rate or an appreciation in the real effective exchange rate or a deterioration of the fiscal position would tend to worsen it.

An improvement in the terms of trade – for example, because of an increase in the export price – increases the value of net exports and this tends to improve the current account position. An increase in the export price may also encourage a transfer of resources from the non-tradable sector to the tradable sector, leading to an increase in the supply of export products. On the other hand, favourable terms of trade may be accompanied by real exchange rate appreciation, leading to deterioration in the current account position. The overall impact depends on the relative magnitude of the first and second effects.

An increase in the growth rate of the industrial countries affects the current account through two channels. The first channel arises from an increase in the demand for the exports of the domestic economy. This increase tends to increase the current account position. Second, an improvement in the economic situation in the developed countries will be associated with an outward shift of the demand for the domestic country exports, with positive impact on the current account through improvements in the terms of trade.

An increase in foreign interest rates would tend to increase the cost of new external debt and the servicing of outstanding debt, and would increase the current account deficit. An appreciation of the real effective exchange rate reduces the competitiveness of the tradable sector, leading to a reduction in exports and current account deterioration. An increase in fiscal deficit that is financed through monetary expansion has the effect of increasing aggregate demand, with a negative impact on the current account balance.

6.3 Traditional Models of Current Account Determination: Empirical Results for Nigeria

Five macroeconomic variables are used to evaluate the determinants of the current account. The real interest rate (r^*) is defined as the London Interbank Offer Rate (LIBOR) minus the rate of inflation in the industrial countries. The terms of trade (tot) is defined as the unit import price index divided by the export unit index. The real effective exchange rate is as the weighted average of the bilateral real exchange rate. The world output (wo) is captured by an index of industrial countries' output. The fiscal deficit is as defined above. Two dummies are introduced to capture the impact of the oil price shock in 1973 (D1) and the introduction of the Structural Adjustment Program in 1986 (D2). The Nigerian data on the variables used for the empirical estimation of (6.12) are provided in the Data Appendix at the end of the chapter.

We examined for Nigeria the current account, terms of trade, world output, world interest rate, real effective exchange rate, and the fiscal deficits for the presence of unit roots. Of these variables, we found, using the Augmented Dickey Fuller and Phillip-Perron Tests, that the current account and the fiscal deficits as a ratio of GDP were stationary. The rest of the variables are first-difference stationary at the 5 percent significance level. The time plots of these variables are shown in Figure 6.1, while Tables 6.1 and 6.2 summarize the ADF and PP unit root tests. The results reported from applying the ADF and PP tests include a constant and a time trend. The presence or absence of unit roots in the variables of interest is not sensitive to the number of lags included.

In estimating (6.12) for Nigeria, we use changes in the terms of trade, the real exchange rate and the terms of trade, given the fact that their levels are nonstationary. The terms of trade show a significant negative relationship with the current account, indicating that a rise in the import price of goods being imported into Nigeria will be associated with current account deterioration. The coefficient on the real interest rate is negative and significant, as expected. The growth rate for industrial countries does not appear to impact significantly on the Nigerian current account; hence we exclude it from the results reported in Table 6.3. This partly reflects the small share of manufactured goods in the Nigerian GNP. Import demand increased persistently in the 1970s, following the increase in the international oil price, thereby reducing the sensitivity of the current account balance to the evolution of the industrial countries' output. After the fall in oil prices, the restrictive trade policy measures initiated by the Nigerian government (tightening of exchange controls and quantitative restrictions) were quite effective in offsetting the direct effects of the economic deterioration in industrial countries. The fiscal balance has a positive and significant relationship with the current account balance; indicating that an increase in fiscal deficits in the context of the Nigerian economy is associated with deterioration in the current account balance. This observed positive relationship between the increase in fiscal deficits and the current account deterioration is easily explained in the context of the Nigerian economy. In the aftermath of the significant fall in oil prices, instead of allowing the real exchange rate to absorb the shock and thereby remove external imbalance, the Nigerian government resorted to the use of international credit markets for additional funds to maintain the unsustainable consumption levels. In addition, the budget deficits of the 1980s were monetised, thus expanding private spending and extending the adverse effects on the current account. The coefficient on the change in the real exchange rate suggests that appreciation in the real exchange rate has had a negative and significant impact on the current account. Overall, both the oil price shock of 1973 and the introduction of the Structural Adjustment Program in 1986 have had significant positive impact on Nigeria's current account during the period considered by this book, as reflected in positive and significant coefficients on D1 (oil price shock) and D2 (Structural Adjustment Program Shock); the two dummies are jointly significant. The diagnostic statistics suggest the absence of serial correlation, non-normality and heteroscedasticity as shown in the respective LM, J-B (probability) ARCH statistics reported in Table 6.3.

It must be noted that arguments provided by the traditional models of the current account are used to characterize the relationship between the current account and its determinants. However, the intertemporal model can also be used to characterize this observed relationship.

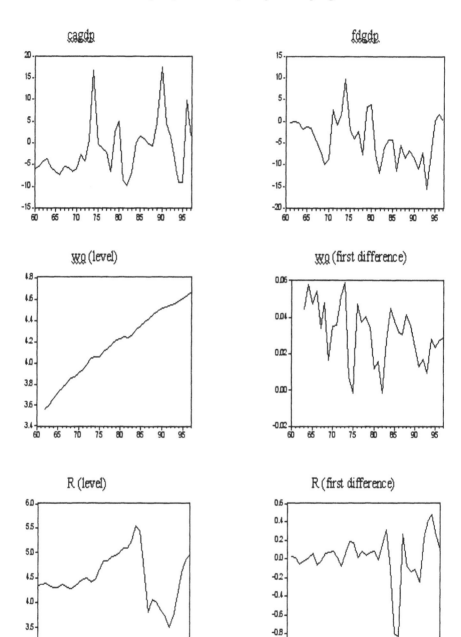

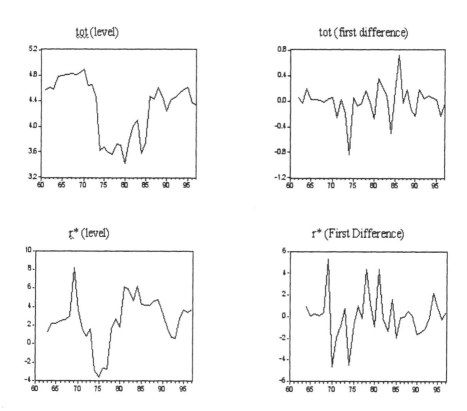

Figure 6.1   Graphical Representation for Nigeria of the Determinants of the Current Account

Table 6.1   Unit Root Tests for Nigeria

Variable	ADF*	PP*
Current Account/GDP (cagdp)	-4.10	-4.16
Terms of Trade (tot)	-1.69	-1.70
World output (wo)	-2.98	-2.98
World Interest Rate (r*)	-2.20	-2.38
Real Effective Exchange Rate (R)	-2.62	-1.77
Fiscal Deficit/GDP (fdgdp)	-3.20	-3.57

* ADF indicates the Augmented Dickey-Fuller test; PP represents the Phillip-Perron test.

Table 6.2   Unit Root Tests for Nigeria

Variable (First Difference)	ADF*	PP*
Terms of Trade	-4.8	-5.7
World output	-4.3	-4.4
World Interest Rate	-4.5	-6.3
Real Effective Exchange Rate	-4.2	-3.7

* ADF indicates the Augmented Dickey-Fuller test; PP represents the Phillip-Perron test.

6.4 Comparisons of the PVMCA and the Traditional Models of the Current Account

From the PVMCA perspective, the current account balance reflects the outcome of optimising decisions by private, forward-looking economic agents. The PVMCA presented in chapter 4 identified expected changes in net output, exchange rate, terms of trade and the interest rate as the determinants of the current account. However, the traditional approaches perceive the current account deficit as resulting from real exchange rate appreciation and excess money supply. They view observation of current account deficit as requiring a policy adjustment, either through nominal exchange rate devaluation or through a contraction of the money supply.

The objectives of this section are twofold. First, we demonstrate that the results from empirical estimation of (6.12) can be explained by the PVMCA as well, focusing on government expenditures and the terms of trade. Second, we establish criteria that can be used to choose between the traditional models of the current account and the PVMCA.

6.5 Comparing the Predictions of the PVMCA and of the Traditional Models

The Impact of Increases in Government Expenditures

The traditional approach uses the monetary, elasticities and absorption approaches to explain the impact of an increase in government expenditure on the current account. An increase in government expenditure financed by monetary expansion generates an increase in liquidity leading to an increase in aggregate demand for both domestic and foreign goods. This results in deterioration of the current account balance. First, the nature of the impact that a temporary change in government expenditure will have on the current account will depend on whether the change is expected or not. An unexpected increase in government expenditure reduces resources available to the private sector for consumption. To smooth consumption, the government borrows abroad in order to maintain the same level of consumption, which leads to a deterioration in the current account balance. However, if the change is expected, the agents reduce their current consumption and this results in a current account surplus in the current period. The PVMCA can explain an observed positive relationship between the current account deficit and the fiscal deficit. The increase in fiscal deficits with negative impact on the current account is consistent with the traditional models of the current account. This indicates that an increase in government expenditure financed by monetary accommodation would generate an increase in absorption and lead to a current account deficit. However, an unexpected temporary increase in government expenditure would produce deterioration in the current account position. This shows that results from empirical implementation of (6.12) cannot be used as bases for choosing between the PVMCA and the traditional models of the current account.

Table 6.3   Nigeria: Dependent Variable, Current Account as a ratio of GDP (cagdp)*

Regressors	Coefficient	Std. errors
Constant	-3.978	1.280
Change in Terms of Trade (tot)	-0.259	0.050
Change in World Interest Rate (r*)	-0.728	0.359
Change in Real Effective Exchange Rate (R)	-0.093	0.026
Fiscal Deficit/GDP (fdgdp)	0.355	0.136
D1 (Structural Adjustment)	4.520	1.596
D2 (Oil shock)	3.588	1.687

$R^2 = 0.67$; F-statistic = 12.42; AR (2) = 0.84; ARCH (1) = 0.81; N (2) = 0.53

*   AR (2), ARCH (1), and N (2) are the standard LM test for no second order serial correlation under the null, the LM tests for the maintained hypothesis of no first order conditional heteroscedasticity and the Jarque-Berra test for normality respectively. Only the corresponding *p-values* of these tests are reported.

The Impact of Terms of Trade Changes

A temporary appreciation in the terms of trade has an ambiguous impact on the current account within the context of the PVMCA. On the one hand, the 'consumption-smoothing' motive implies that agents will maintain the same level of spending in the event of a temporary increase in the real income. This induces an improvement in the current account balance if the temporary appreciation in the terms of trade takes place in the current period and is unexpected. However, this same appreciation will lead to an improvement in the current account balance if it is anticipated to take place in the future.

Apart from this income effect, there are also intertemporal and intratemporal substitution effects. First, a temporary unexpected current (expected future) appreciation in the terms of trade reduces (increases) the cost of current consumption in terms of future consumption. This fall (rise) in the consumption-based real interest rate, when associated with temporary current (expected future) improvements in the terms of trade, discourages (increases) saving and hence engenders a deterioration in the current account in the case of a current shock, but a worsening of the current account position in the case of a future shock. This is the intertemporal substitution effect. Second, a temporary change in the terms of trade changes both the level and composition of aggregate real spending, of which nontradable goods are included. A current unanticipated improvement in the terms of trade implies an increase in the price of tradable goods relative to the nontradable goods. Economic agents, in response, will shift toward consuming nontradable goods and this will produce an increase in the price of nontradable goods, leading to a real exchange rate appreciation and a negative impact on the current account. If the improvement in the price of tradables is anticipated, then the current price of tradable goods is relatively cheaper compared to that of nontradables. Agents will thus shift towards consuming tradable goods, which will lead to a fall in the price of nontradable goods and then to a real exchange rate depreciation and a consequent improvement in the current account. This clearly shows that the impact on the current account of changes in the terms of trade depends on whether it is anticipated or not. Moreover, the overall impact of changes in the terms of trade depends on the relative strength of the consumption smoothing intertemporal and intratemporal effects.

In the traditional model, an increase in the terms of trade increases the export price relative to the import price and, given static identity, this improves the current account balance. There is no indication as to whether the change in the terms of trade is expected or not. Both the traditional approach and the PVMCA can explain a finding of negative relationship between the current account and the terms of trade, as reported in section 6.4.

This section has shown that that the way in which the PVMCA and the traditional model establish a linkage between an economic variable and current account is quite different, especially as these different ways reflect the issue of expectation. The difficulty is to interpret empirical regularity in the data; both the traditional models and the PVMCA can explain an observed relationship between a macro variable and the current account.

Choosing between the PVMCA and the Traditional Models

A difficulty with the estimation of (6.12) is that, depending on how we want to explain these results, the results could be considered as consistent with any of the models. An alternative would be to decompose each of the variables into their permanent and temporary components; however, the earlier literature on the intertemporal approach indicates that this can be difficult. To illustrate, Ahmed (1986) decomposed government expenditures into temporary and permanent components and found that temporary changes in government expenditures and not the permanent changes are important for the current account. Obstfeld and Rogoff (1994), using a cross section of 15 OECD countries found that neither current nor permanent government spending is important in explaining the behaviour of the current account balance. They interpret the results to indicate that it is not clear whether the intertemporal approach is simply invalid, or whether the many extraneous simplifications and maintained hypotheses imposed by the econometrician are to blame. Moreover, Cardia (1997) replicated standard consumption function tests of the Ricardian equivalence using series generated from a model which nests Ricardian equivalence within a non-Ricardian alternative. She found that no conclusion could be drawn from the observation of a low correlation between the current account and government budget deficits. All these findings point to the fact that the empirical results obtained from estimating

(6.12) cannot be used as bases for choosing between the intertemporal model and the traditional models of the current account.

There are a number of factors favouring the use of the PVMCA rather than traditional approaches. An important issue is the optimal dynamic responses of savings and investment to external and internal shocks. The traditional models of the current account are not designed to deal with this issue; it can, however, be dealt with in the context of the PVMCA.

Another important point in favour of the PVMCA is Lucas' (1976) position that policy analysis must be based on actual forward-looking decision rules of economic agents. Obstfeld and Rogoff (1994) interpreted this as implying that open-economy models based on the optimization problems of a household may yield more reliable policy conclusions than *ad hoc* econometric specification such as demonstrated by equation (6.12).

Another advantage of a microeconomic foundation is that it imposes more structure on the macro model. Consequently, the corresponding empirical work involves fewer 'free' parameters (parameters that are not constrained by theoretical considerations and can thus take on whatever value that will maximize the fit of the model). Since the variables entering the empirical estimation of the PVMCA are theoretically derived, this restricts the number of variables that could enter the estimation.

Given the issues examined in this book – the solvency of the economy and the excessiveness and sustainability of current account deficits, the use of the PVMCA appears more appropriate. As earlier indicated in this chapter, the PVMCA provides a framework for analysing the excessiveness of the current account current account deficits. Second, addressing the issue of the economy's solvency is an intertemporal issue, given the fact that the PVMCA has an intertemporal underpinnings, this makes it more appealing relative to the traditional approaches.

6.6 Additional Indicators of Current Account Deficits Sustainability

Chapter 2 presented a number of macroeconomic variables that can be used to assess the sustainability of the external position of an economy. In tracing the evolution of the Nigerian economy during the period 1960-97, we discovered in Chapter 2, a remarkable current account deficit, an increase in external debt GDP ratio, a sharp real exchange rate appreciation, low economic growth, a sharp increase in fiscal deficits and a drastic fall in foreign exchange reserves in the periods before the external crisis of 1986. This section focuses on additional indicators of current account deficits sustainability. We look at the following variables: capital flight, openness and trade composition, composition of current account balance, and political instability.

Capital Flight

A relevant factor in assessing the external position of a country is the size of the potential capital flight. Higher levels of capital flight during certain periods may reflect anticipations of devaluation, fiscal deficits, inflation, and financial repression culminating in a negative real interest rates and political instability. Hence, capital flight is a summary indicator that reflects the degree of economic distortion and is relevant for assessing whether the country is likely to experience an external crisis or not.

Given the relative importance of capital in a capital-scarce economy like Nigeria, the most relevant definition of capital flight is one that unifies the "sources and uses" of capital (Ajayi, 1995). Given this condition, we use the World Bank (1985) definition of capital flight.[5] The definition of capital flight from the World Bank (1985) perspective is given by:

$$KF = CD + NFD + CAB + CIR \qquad (6.13)$$

where KF is the capital flight, CD is the change in external debt, NFD is net foreign direct investment, CAB represents the current account balance and CIR is the change in official reserves. Equation (6.13) implies that any inflows that do not finance direct foreign investment and official reserve increases leave the country in the form of capital flight.

We use the estimate of capital flight derived from (6.13) to gauge the extent of illegal capital outflows for Nigeria before 1986. Figure 6.2 shows the evolution of capital flight from Nigeria during the period 1972-97. There were dramatic changes over the period 1972-97. Capital flight stood at an annual average of US$496 million during 1972-79, increased to US$1,478 million in the pre-crisis period (1980-86) and then to US$3,071 million during 1987-94. This points to higher capital flight preceding the external crisis. Macroeconomic instability might have produced the increase in the capital flight during the period 1987-1994. However, a reversal in capital flows took place during 1995-97.[6]

Composition of Capital Inflows

The sustainability of current account deficits depends on how they are financed: direct foreign investment (FDI), portfolio investment (equity securities, debt securities), loans and trade deficits. A current account deficit financed through FDI, for instance, is likely to be more sustainable as it does not create debt and contributes to the

---

[5] There exists a huge literature on various approaches to measuring capital flight. Our focus is on examining the evolution of the capital fight for Nigeria and to see whether it increased tremendously before the crisis year 1986.

[6] Estimates of capital flight were negative in some years. This reflects capital flight net of unrecorded capital inflow (Cuddington, 1986) and these years can be considered as years of capital repatriation.

economy's growth potential. It is therefore, important, to examine the source of financing current account deficits.

For Nigeria, foreign direct investment was the major source of financing current account deficits over the period 1960-73. This was also the case up to 1979 (Figure 6.3). Over the period 1982-85, which preceded the external crisis, the short-term capital inflows emerged as the major source of financing current account deficits. The change in the composition of capital inflows reflected the lack of confidence in the Nigerian economy by foreign investors and their anticipation of a possible external crisis.

In more recent years, there is evidence of significant outflows of capital, as shown by persistent net short-term capital outflows. In a capital-scarce economy like Nigeria, one would have expected a net inflow. This is not to suggest that a country is better off financing its current account deficits through short-term capital inflows, but simply to note that persistent capital outflows tend to suggest the existence of structural problems. The political uncertainty over the period 1992-97 is the likely reason for the net outflows.

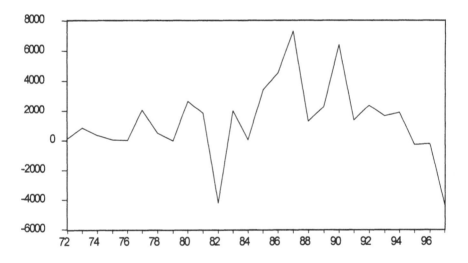

Figure 6.2   Nigeria: Capital Flight, 1972-97 (US $million)

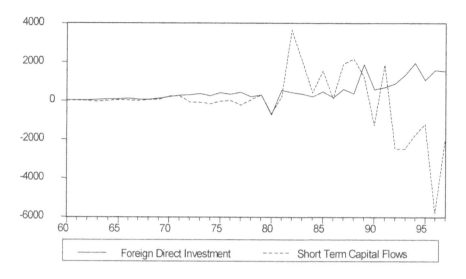

Figure 6.3   Nigeria: Foreign Direct Investment and Short-Term Capital Inflow, 1960-97 ($US millions)

Openness and Trade Composition

A more open economy (with a higher exports-GDP ratio) is expected to generate higher foreign exchange earnings, and is in a better position to service its external debt. Nonetheless, a high degree of openness could increase the vulnerability of the country to external crises, especially when the export base is thin. An economy that has a diversified export base may not experience an external crisis as a result of a fall in the terms of trade for a particular export category. However, an economy that derives a significant portion of its export earnings from one product may suffer an external crisis in the event of a fall in its relative price.

The degree of external orientation, as measured by the ratio of exports to GDP, increased considerably for Nigeria over the 1960-97 period from an annual average of 10 percent in the 1960s to 18 percent in the 70s, 21 percent in the 80s and 43 percent in the 90s (Figure 6.4).

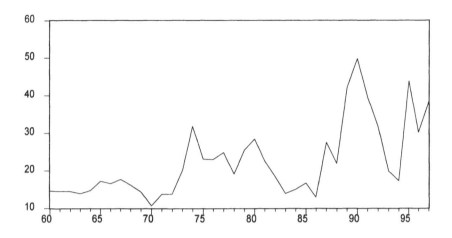

Figure 6.4   Nigeria: Export to GDP Ratio (1960-97)

The increased export-GDP ratio was combined with high dependence on oil receipts and this tended to increase the vulnerability of the Nigerian economy to developments in the world oil markets. The share of oil receipts in total exports was on average 19 percent in the 1960s, 86 percent in the 1970s and 1980s, and 90 percent in the 1990s. The immense dependence on oil exports shows that a given current account position that may be ordinarily considered to be sustainable may easily deteriorate to an unsustainable path given an unexpected fall in the world oil prices.

Political Instability and Policy Uncertainty

Political instability negatively affects the level of investment and consequent growth and thus bears on the ability of the country to service its debt. For this reason, we have included this variable in assessing the sustainability of current-account deficits.

In the context of current-account sustainability, political instability can be relevant, since it subjects domestic and foreign investors to the risk of a sudden policy reversal, reducing the credibility of the current policy stance. Replacement of a government favouring free capital mobility by one prone to the imposition of capital controls makes the occurrence of capital outflows more likely.

Nigeria has experienced considerable political instability. Its system of governance has oscillated between military regimes and civilian administrations. This political instability produced instability in the macroeconomic policy stance of the government. If we assess external sustainability on the basis of this indicator, Nigeria does not fare well. The country experienced civil war over the period 1967-70. The military took over from the civilians in 1983 and assumed control over the Nigerian economy up to the end of the period covered by this study. There were a series of coups and counter-coups. This political turmoil did not favour the inflow of foreign resources, but rather encouraged capital flight.

6.7 Solvency and Resource Balance Gaps

Solvency can be established by making use of the following relationship between the change in the net foreign assets position of a country and the current account balance:

$$(1+r^*)B_t = C_t + G_t + I_t - Y_t + B_{t+1} \tag{6.14}$$

where r^* is the constant world interest rate; B is the net foreign assets; C is private consumption, G is government expenditures, I is private and government investment expenditures and Y is gross domestic product. Shifting (6.14) forward by one period and dividing through by $(1+r^*)$ yields:

$$B_{t+1} = \frac{C_{t+1} + G_{t+1} + I_{t+1} - Y_{t+1}}{1+r^*} + \frac{B_{t+2}}{1+r^*} \tag{6.15}$$

Dividing both sides of (6.14) by $(1+r^*)^2$ and shifting the result forward by two periods in order to eliminate $B_{t+2}/1+r^*$ from (6.15), we obtain:

$$\frac{B_{t+2}}{(1+r^*)} = \frac{C_{t+2} + G_{t+2} + I_{t+2} - Y_{t+2}}{(1+r^*)^2} + \frac{B_{t+3}}{(1+r^*)^2} \tag{6.16}$$

From (6.16), the current net foreign assets are given by:

$$B_t = -\left[\frac{Y_t - C_t - G_t - I_t}{1+r^*} + \frac{Y_{t+1} - C_{t+1} - G_{t+1} - I_{t+1}}{(1+r^*)^2} + \frac{B_{t+2}}{(1+r^*)^2} \right] \tag{6.17}$$

By following this iterative substitution, successive values of B_{t+i} can be eliminated. For ease of exposition, assume that we are interested in a two-period analysis. Assume $B_{t+2} = 0$, i.e., any external debt is paid off by the end of (t+2) and there are no foreign assets. The elimination of B_{t+2} from (6.17) based on this condition implies that:

$$B_t = -\left[\frac{NX_t}{1+r^*} + \frac{NX_{t+1}}{(1+r^*)^2} \right] \tag{6.18}$$

where $Y - C - G - I = NX$ and NX is net exports inclusive of services.

In a two-period analysis, (6.18) is the solvency condition; it indicates that the present value of net exports must be equal to the current indebtedness. Extending (6.18) to an infinite horizon and taking its mathematical expectation produces:

$$E_\tau \{(1+r^*)B_\tau\} = -\left[E_\tau \left\{ \sum_{t=\tau}^{\infty} \left(\frac{1}{1+r^*} \right)^{t-\tau} (Y_t - C_t - I_t - G_t) - \left(\frac{1}{1+r^*} \right)^T B_{\tau+T+1} \right\} \right]$$

(6.19)

The assumption of non-satiation prevents B_{t+2} from being positive (the rest of the world does not owe the economic agents in the domestic economy at the end of the period) and *no Ponzi* game constraint prevents it from being negative (agents cannot owe the rest of the world at the end of the game). As in the two-period case:

$$Lim\ T \to \infty \left(\frac{1}{1+r^*} \right)^T B_{\tau+T+1} = 0$$

Hence, (6.19) becomes:

$$E_\tau \{(1+r^*)B_\tau\} = -\left[E_\tau \left\{ \sum_{t=\tau}^{\infty} \left(\frac{1}{1+r^*} \right)^{t-\tau} (NX_t) \right\} \right]$$

(6.20)

Now divide both sides of (6.20) by (1+r*), so that we can solve for B_τ. This yields:

$$B_\tau = -\left\{ \sum_{t=\tau}^{\infty} \frac{1}{1+r^*} \left(\frac{1}{1+r^*} \right)^{t-\tau} (E_\tau NX_t) \right\}$$

(6.21)

Equation (6.21) can be re-written so that it is similar to the case of the two period analyses, this yields:

$$B_\tau = -\left\{ \sum_{t=\tau}^{\infty} \left(\frac{1}{1+r^*} \right)^{t-\tau-1} (E_\tau NX_t) \right\}$$

(6.22)

Equation (6.22) has the same interpretation as (6.18) – that is, an economy is considered to be solvent as long as it can generate sufficient net exports surpluses in the future to meet pre-existing external obligation as captured by B_τ.

As noted in Chapter 2, using the solvency condition to assess the external position of an economy has a number of limitations. First, there is uncertainty in forecasting the ability of a country to generate sufficient future trade surpluses to repay the current debt obligations. Second, solvency does not distinguish between the ability and the willingness to pay and lend. Therefore, instead of working with the solvency condition, we use an established 'test' of the solvency condition, which is a non-increasing external debt to GDP ratio. A country is likely to remain solvent as long as the ratio is not growing.

Milesi-Ferretti and Razin (1996) demonstrated that a non-increasing external debt GDP ratio is a function of the real interest rate, real growth rate of domestic output, changes in the real exchange rate and the net exports. The equation capturing this relationship is presented in (6.23):

$$b_t - b_{t-1} = nx_t + \frac{(1+r^*) - (1+g_t)(1+\varepsilon_t)}{(1+g_t)(1+\varepsilon_t)} b_{t-1} \qquad (6.23)^7$$

where b_t is now the stock of foreign assets denominated in foreign goods. The ratio of foreign assets to output (b_t) equals $B_t/q_t Y_t$; q_t is the real exchange rate; r^* is the real world interest rate, g is the growth rate and ε is the rate of real appreciation. From (6.23), changes in the ratio of foreign assets to GDP are driven by both trade imbalances (nx_t) and a 'debt dynamics' term that is positively related to the world real rate of interest and negatively related to the rate of real exchange rate appreciation and the rate of domestic economic growth.

It is important to determine the long term net resource transfer (positive net exports) required to maintain a constant net foreign assets output ratio. To achieve this, we assume that, at the steady state, the net foreign asset position remains constant. Based on constant net foreign assets as a ratio of real output, the net resource transfer (nx_t) required to stabilize the ratio of net foreign assets to output is given by:

$$nx = -\frac{(1+r^*) - (1+g_t)(1+\varepsilon_t)}{(1+g_t)(1+\varepsilon_t)} b \qquad (6.24)$$

where nx is the long-term net exports. The resource balance gap is the difference between the net exports required to stabilize the net foreign assets GDP ratio and the actual current net exports (both as percentages of GDP). Using (6.24), the sustainability of the current account position of a country can be carried out. If the net exports required stabilizing the net foreign assets as a ratio of output is greater than the currently observed net exports, this indicates unsustainability and calls for a policy change such as a devaluation of the currency in order to boost exports and reduce imports. Furthermore, (6.24) adds another twist to analysing the sustainability of the external position of a country. It may be the case that a country is experiencing a current account surplus but the observed surplus may not be

---

[7] See Milesi-Ferretti and Razin (1996, p. 10).

sufficient to ensure a stable net foreign asset output ratio. In such a situation, despite a positive current account balance, it may be necessary to further enhance the current account position so as to ensure that the intertemporal solvency condition is satisfied.

We assume different scenarios in order to establish which current account path will likely ensure a constant debt to GDP ratio. In all the scenarios considered, the expected exchange rate depreciation[8] is taken to be zero and, as a result, the equation for calculating the current account surplus required to stabilize the external debt GDP ratio reduces to:

$$nx = -\frac{r^* - g_t}{(1 + g_t)}b \qquad (6.25)$$

Under the first scenario (Table 6.4), we report the current account surplus that stabilizes the external debt GDP ratio at its pre-crisis (1985) level of 66 percent, given varying assumptions about the real growth rate and the real international interest rate. Using the annual average growth rate of 3 percent during the period 1961-85, and an assumed real international interest rate of 4 percent, the goods and services deficit (inclusive of transfers) required to maintain a constant external debt GDP ratio as of 1985 was 0.67 percent. In order to assess the external position of the Nigerian economy before the occurrence of an external crisis in 1986, this ratio was compared with the average of the net trade balance inclusive of services and transfers during the period 1981-83.[9] The actual average of net trade balance during the period 1981-83 was -6.33 percent of GDP. This indicates a resource gap of about -7 percent of GDP.

As indicated above, the current account balance (excluding interest payments) that ensures a constant external debt to GDP ratio is 0.67. This implies that to maintain a constant external debt to GDP ratio in the future, the goods and services surplus (inclusive of transfers) must average 0.67 percent of GDP. Given the outstanding cost of external debt, the calculated interest payment on servicing external debt equals about 2.64 percent of GDP. The overall annual current account deficit of -1.97 percent of GDP is permissible. In the event that the Nigerian economy is able to achieve a higher growth rate of 5 percent, with a real international rate of 4 percent, the trade balance inclusive of services and transfers must average a deficit of -0.67 of GDP and the economy can afford an overall deficit of about 3.31 percent of GDP.

---

[8]   This assumption is consistent with Corsetti *et al.* (1998) and Obstfeld and Rogoff (1994).

[9]   This is the case, because the government put in place austerity measures and strict exchange and import controls that appeared to reduce the imports of goods and services during the 1984-85 period.

Table 6.4   Scenarios of Nigeria's Current Account Position

Real Interest Rate (percent)	Scenario 1 (Stabilize Debt-GDP ratio) Growth Rate of Real Income			Scenario 1 (Reducing Debt-GDP ratio) Growth Rate of Real Income		
	3%	5%	7%	3%	5%	7%
2.00	-0.66	-1.98	-3.30	-0.33	-0.99	-1.65
3.00	0.00	-1.32	-2.64	0.00	-0.66	-1.32
4.00	0.66	-1.32	-2.64	0.33	-0.66	-1.32
5.00	1.32	0.00	-1.32	0.66	0.00	-0.66
6.00	1.98	0.66	0.00	0.99	0.33	0.00

In the period 1986-97, the actual current account surplus averaged about 1.5 percent of GDP, which is higher than the required current account balance of 0.67. However, increasing the real interest rate, interest expenditure on outstanding debt stock. or a reduction in the growth rate would change this conclusion. Table 6.4 presents various scenarios pointing to the fact that a higher growth rate for the Nigerian economy augments its ability to increase its current account deficits without increasing the external debt to GDP ratio. On the other hand, higher interest rates lower the ability of the Nigerian economy to have a larger current account deficit that will be sustainable.

6.8 Excessiveness of the Current Account Balances

From Chapters 4 and 5, the equation for the optimal current account balance, with changes in the interest rate and exchange rate (with asymmetry excluded) is given by:

$$hz_t = -\sum_{t=\tau+1}^{\infty} \beta^{t-\tau}(g_1 - \gamma g_2)\Psi^{t-\tau} z_t \qquad (6.26)$$

The variables in (6.26) are defined as follows: $z_t = (cneo_t \; ca_t \; \hat{r}_t)$, $g_1 = [1\;0\;0]$, $g_2 = [0\;0\;1]$, and $h = [0\;1\;0]$ and $\hat{r}_t$ is the consumption-based interest rate that includes the world real interest rate, and expected change in the exchange rate. Equation (6.26) is re-written as:

$$ca_t^{**} = kz_t \qquad (6.27)$$
$$k = -(g_1 - \gamma g_2)\,\beta\Psi(I - \beta\Psi)^{-1}$$

As we are interested in examining the excessiveness of the current account deficits, possible asymmetry in access becomes important. As was established in Chapter 5, there is evidence that a restriction of asymmetry in access to the international financial markets cannot be rejected. We therefore focus on two optimal current accounts – optimal current account that reflects asymmetry and the one that does not. The optimal current account (with asymmetry in access to the international financial market) is given by:

$$hz_t = -\sum_{t=\tau+1}^{\infty} \beta^{t-\tau}(g_1 - \gamma g_2)\Psi^{t-\tau} z_t \qquad (6.28)$$

where $z_t = (\,cneo_t^h \;\; cneo_t^l \;\; ca_t^h \;\; ca_t^l \;\; \hat{r}_t\,)'$, $g_1 = [1\ 1\ 0\ 0\ 0]$, $g_2 = [0\ 0\ 0\ 0\ 1]$, and $h = [0\ 0\ 1\ 1\ 0]$. Re-expressing (5.6), we have:

$$ca_t{}^{****} = kz_t \qquad (6.29)$$

where $k = -(g_1 - \gamma g_2)\beta\Psi(I - \beta\Psi)^{-1}$.

We employ the value of 0.45 for the intertemporal elasticity, γ and we use 0.85 for the share of the tradable goods. The PVMCA is then used to assess the excessiveness of the Nigerian current account imbalances before the year 1986. The actual current account, and estimates of the optimal current account without asymmetry in access (changes in interest rates and exchange rates considered – optimal 2), and the current account in the face of asymmetry in access (optimal 5) are shown in Figure 6.5. For most of the period, the three current account balances were in deficit. The first important observation is that, for most of these years, the actual current account balances could be considered excessive relative to either the constrained or unconstrained current account. In the period before 1986, especially 1981-83, the current account balances were persistently excessive. The strict trade and exchange policy measures curbed this trend during 1984-85. However, the unsustainability of such policy measures was reflected in a dramatic widening of the gap between the optimal and actual current account balance in 1986.

Finally, for most of the years, the optimal current account deficit, in the absence of unrestricted access to the international financial market, is greater than that of the optimal current account that allows for possible asymmetry. This is a further confirmation of the fact that in the face of unexpected shocks, the economic agents in Nigeria would not be able to use the international financial markets to the extent they desired.

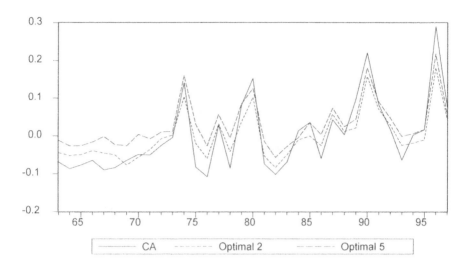

Figure 6.5 Nigeria: Actual and Optimal Current Accounts (Unrestricted and Restricted Access)

Conclusions

This chapter has used macroeconomic indicators to examine the external position of the Nigerian economy over the 1960-97 periods. In view of the empirical results for this economy, we note the following observations. First, current account surpluses achieved by stringent exchange controls can still produce external crises due to adverse external shocks. This reflects the fact that current account surpluses arising from exchange controls do not address the fundamental causes of the problems and are, therefore, not sustainable. In the same vein, it is crucial to examine whether the observed current account surpluses are sufficient to ensure that the intertemporal solvency condition is satisfied.

Second, and most important for the current study, is the fact that the underlying factors behind a given path of current account balances determines whether they will generate an external crises or not. Although Nigeria had consistent current account deficits over the period 1960-73, there was no evidence of exchange rate depreciation, foreign debt crises, or lack of access to the international financial market. Thus, in spite of the consistent current account deficits over that period, there was no occurrence of external crises. However, the external imbalances over the 1981-85 period culminated in an external crisis in the form of exchange rate depreciation and foreign debt crisis.[10] There was also a considerable amount of resource gap during the same period.

The use of various indicators to assess the sustainability of the Nigerian current account deficits allows additional insight. An assessment of the sustainability of external imbalances must be based on a wide range of relevant macroeconomic indicators. Current account deficits associated with exchange rate appreciations and fiscal deficits appear not to be sustainable. Current account deficits that are associated with low savings, a high concentration of exports in a particular commodity, lower economic growth, growing external debt, high debt servicing, inadequate foreign exchange reserves and political instability could degenerate into external crises.

It is important to note that the PVMCA is able to establish for Nigeria the excessiveness of current account deficits in most of the years covered by this book: for most of the years, the actual current account balances were excessive relative to the optimal current accounts. For Nigeria, in the period before 1986, especially between 1981 and 1983, the current account balances were persistently excessive. The strict trade and exchange policy measures curbed this trend during 1984-85. However, the unsustainability of such policy measures was reflected in a dramatic widening of the gap between optimal and actual current account balance in 1986.

Finally, continual use of the floating exchange rate, reduction in fiscal deficits, increased savings rate, diversification of the export base, increased economic performance as measured by the growth rate of the economy, efficient debt management strategy, and political stability must be pursued in Nigeria. This policy package is essential if the country is to sustain deficits that may be associated with increased investment rates in the future. Moreover, by pursuing this policy package consistently, economic agents in Nigeria could have increased access to the international financial markets.

---

[10] This is not to dispute the fact that increased world interest rates and declining terms of trade necessitated the sharp policy reversal of 1986.

Data Appendix 6.I

	Current Account to GDP	Terms of Trade Index (1995=100)	Industrial Countries Output Index (1995=100)	World Real Interest Rate	Real Effect. Exc. Rate	Fiscal Deficits to GDP
1960	-5.80	na	na	na	75.96	na
1961	-5.30	96.09	na	na	77.94	-0.30
1962	-4.20	100.84	35.30	na	79.36	0.00
1963	-3.80	97.15	36.90	0.93	74.93	-0.40
1964	-5.60	118.29	39.10	1.72	73.55	-1.70
1965	-6.50	120.24	41.00	1.85	74.03	-1.40
1966	-7.30	122.81	43.30	2.25	78.33	-1.60
1967	-5.50	123.50	44.80	2.24	73.53	-4.40
1968	-5.70	121.77	47.00	2.70	71.84	-6.70
1969	-6.70	125.63	47.80	7.65	75.66	-9.90
1970	-5.90	132.83	49.50	3.64	81.26	-8.70
1971	-2.60	102.45	51.30	1.68	87.89	2.60
1972	-4.20	104.17	54.00	0.81	88.67	-0.80
1973	0.50	86.19	57.30	2.01	81.59	1.50
1974	16.70	37.17	57.70	-1.52	86.77	9.80
1975	-0.20	39.35	57.60	-2.66	104.80	-2.00
1976	-1.20	36.25	60.40	-2.05	124.80	-4.00
1977	-2.10	35.23	62.70	-2.14	125.74	-2.40
1978	-6.70	41.48	65.30	1.97	135.53	-7.80
1979	2.40	40.86	67.60	3.39	140.07	3.40
1980	5.00	30.79	68.40	2.87	150.29	3.90
1981	-8.50	44.03	69.50	7.01	162.70	-7.70
1982	-9.90	55.36	69.40	6.35	161.76	-11.80
1983	-6.50	59.92	71.30	4.63	187.63	-5.90
1984	0.10	35.88	74.60	6.21	254.79	-4.20
1985	1.60	42.45	77.50	4.14	230.63	-4.20
1986	1.00	87.13	80.00	3.78	103.81	-11.30
1987	-0.30	83.74	82.50	3.84	44.87	-5.40
1988	-0.80	99.81	86.00	4.41	58.12	-8.40
1989	4.60	87.13	89.10	4.69	53.92	-6.70
1990	17.50	68.72	91.30	3.21	47.23	-8.50
1991	4.40	82.00	92.50	1.63	42.11	-11.00
1992	1.60	85.30	94.10	0.35	32.86	-7.20
1993	-3.70	92.50	95.00	0.22	40.95	-15.50
1994	-9.00	97.86	97.70	2.30	62.11	-7.70

	Current Account to GDP	Terms of Trade Index (1995=100)	Industrial Countries Output Index (1995=100)	World Real Interest Rate	Real Effect. Exc. Rate	Fiscal Deficits to GDP
1995	-9.20	100.00	100.00	3.20	100.00	0.10
1996	9.90	79.17	102.80	2.91	129.33	1.60
1997	1.40	76.31	105.80	5.86	143.68	0.20

Sources: IMF: International Financial Statistics database, Oshikoya (1990).

Chapter 7

An Overview of the Ghanaian Economy

Introduction

This part of the book complements our researches on the current account of the Nigerian economy with those for the Ghanaian economy. Nigeria and Ghana are the two largest economies in West Africa and both are English speaking and share certain patterns of international linkages and institutional arrangements, so that covering them together in this study seemed especially worthwhile. Their comparison also allows a more extensive judgment to be made on the applicability of the Present Value Approach to the Current Account (PVMCA). The underlying theory and the econometric techniques for the PVMCA have already been laid out in the earlier chapters and do not need repetition in this chapter. Therefore, this part of the book focuses on economic and political developments in Ghana during 1957-2000 and the applicability of the PVMCA to the Ghanaian economy.

This chapter presents an overview of the performance of the economy along with developments in the external sector, and the macroeconomic policies pursued since Ghana's independence in 1957. The entire period is divided into two sub-periods; the pre-Economic Recovery Program (ERP) and Structural Adjustment Period (1957-1982); and the post-ERP and Structural Adjustment Period (1983-2000). This separation is justified on the grounds that macroeconomic policies and trade and payments regimes followed in the two sub-periods are distinctively different and that economic developments showed a different pattern as well. Section 7.1, therefore, discusses the association between macroeconomic policies and the performances of both the domestic and the external sectors of the Ghanaian economy during the period leading up to the stabilization program. It also examines the performance of the external sector of the Ghanaian economy and the different trade and payments regimes followed during this period. Section 7.2 does the same for the period after the implementation of the stabilization program.

7.1 Economic Policies: Pre-ERP period (1957-1982)

Ghana's exchange rate and balance of payments policies could be divided into two main periods, the 1957-82 period and that after 1982. The period before 1982 was marked by strict trade controls, a policy pursued by many African countries in order to promote the development of the domestic import-competing firms. This period was also characterized by fixed exchange rates, though with incessant devaluations. The fixed exchange rate regime coupled with accelerating inflation arising from monetization of fiscal deficits, produced real exchange rate appreciation with adverse impact on the exporting sector and encouraged higher level of imports, resulting in unsustainable position of current account deficits. In an attempt to correct the external disequilibrium position, quantitative controls were put in place to discourage imports.

The period from independence in 1957 till the implementation of the stabilization program in 1983 was marked by political instability, with its associated swings in macroeconomic policy stance and trade and payment regimes. The first President of Ghana, Dr. Kwame Nkrumah on assuming office in 1957 maintained the conservative monetary and fiscal policies of the colonial government for a few years before diverting to a more nationalistic approach to development. The five-year post-independence development plan in 1959 focused on accelerated industrialization (import substitution industrialization) that required greater state participation. This led to massive increases in government expenditures. Though the plan was abandoned in 1961, it had already created increasing budget deficits and balance of payment deficits that produced a sharp decline in foreign exchange reserves. In an attempt to solve these problems, the government resorted to a series of measures, prominent among which were austerity budgets, including both cutbacks in expenditures and tax increases. However, increased government capital expenditures led to an overall budget deficit of 7 percent of GDP in 1961 (see Table 7.1). The deficit increased to 9.4 percent in 1962 and further to 9.9 percent in 1963. The seven-year development plan in 1963/64 continued with the general philosophy of import substitution industrialization with further increases in government expenditures. As a result, total government expenditure increased by 36 percent between 1963 and 1965. The budget deficit as a percentage of GDP also increased to 10.9 percent in 1965.

There was evidence of monetary accommodation of fiscal deficits. Between 1960 and 1964, a considerable proportion of the budget deficit was financed by borrowing from the Bank of Ghana and other commercial banks. Government credit as a percentage of total bank credit increased from a low of 6 percent in 1960 to 49 percent in 1965. This led to a large increase in money supply, which more than doubled between 1960 and 1965, with the highest growth rate of 39.5 percent occurring in 1964. Throughout the period the exchange rate was not adjusted and remained fixed at 0.714 Cedis to the US$. Instead, in 1961, the government introduced exchange controls as part of a policy package to control and conserve foreign exchange. We briefly elaborate on the nature of the exchange controls that were introduced by the government and their adverse effects.

Table 7.1 Macroeconomic Policy Indicators

	Growth in money	Budget Deficit*	Deficit to GDP ratio	Exchange Rates	Grants to GDP ratio
1957	-10.6	2.9	0.4	0.714	na
1958	4.8	-12.3	-1.7	0.714	na
1959	12.5	-34.1	-4.2	0.714	na
1960	17.7	-56.8	-6.5	0.714	na
1961	9.3	-112.3	-7.0	0.714	na
1962	12.6	-100.8	-9.4	0.714	na
1963	4.7	-84.8	-9.9	0.714	na
1964	39.5	-79.0	-8.4	0.714	na
1965	-0.2	-94.1	-6.4	0.714	na
1966	3.2	-76.6	-5.0	0.714	na
1967	-2.9	-88.1	-5.9	1.020	na
1968	7.3	-104.0	-6.1	1.020	na
1969	12.0	-66.0	-3.3	1.020	na
1970	5.6	-49.9	-2.2	1.020	na
1971	4.9	-88.4	-3.5	1.818	na
1972	44.1	-161.2	-5.7	1.280	0.114
1973	21.9	-186.6	-5.3	1.150	0.014
1974	23.7	-196.1	-4.2	1.150	0.101
1975	44.6	-401.3	-7.6	1.150	0.017
1976	41.4	-736.2	-11.3	1.150	0.000
1977	67.9	-1056.8	-9.5	1.150	0.271
1978	72.4	-1896.7	-9.0	2.750	0.005
1979	13.4	-1800.0	-6.4	2.750	0.000
1980	30.1	-1808.0	-4.2	2.750	0.000
1981	54.7	-4706.8	-6.5	2.750	0.062
1982	19.0	-4848.0	-5.6	2.750	0.060

* In millions of Ghanaian Cedis.
Sources: IMF: International Financial Statistics; World Bank: World Development
Indicators.

The National Liberation Council (NLC) government came to power in February 1966 and pursued more liberal economic policies. Its main economic and socio-political agenda was to create an economy led by private sector growth. To achieve this, it experimented with trade liberalization and implemented a stabilization program, supported by the IMF and the World Bank, that required fiscal consolidation and prudent monetary policies. In an attempt to reduce the tax burden, various taxes were either reduced or completely abolished. The government also attempted to reduce its expenditures by downsizing the public sector by 5 percent and taking initiatives to cut down on development expenditure through a 16 percent reduction in government capital expenditures in 1969. As reported in Table 7.1, budget deficits as a percentage of GDP improved between 1966 and 1969 when compared with the preceding three years. The aim of monetary policy throughout the years 1966 to 1969 was to contribute towards price stability, without neglecting the specific needs of particular sectors. At the start of each year, specific credit ceilings were prescribed for both the private and government sectors. This was done with the view to reducing growth in money supply. Though growth in money supply was initially controlled, it increased by 12 percent in 1969. As an important adjunct to stabilization measures, as well as a means of solving the deterioration in the balance of payments, the currency was devalued by 43 percent in 1967. The government also introduced price controls.

The civilian government, which had come to power in 1969, initially returned to the earlier nationalistic approach to development but shifted to liberalization policies in 1971. The 1970 budget introduced massive public capital projects, which led to an increase in the government capital expenditures of almost 50 percent between 1969 and 1970. Current expenditures also increased; hence, there was a large increase in overall government expenditures. However, since tax revenues increased substantially due to the overall growth in the economy, the overall budget deficit from 1969 to 1971 was much improved. The budget deficit as a percentage of GDP was 3.3 percent in 1969, and then fell to 2.2 percent in 1970, before increasing again to 3.5 percent in 1971. These figures are by far the lowest the country had seen since its independence in 1957.

In spite of the fiscal achievements, the achievements on the monetary front were less impressive. There was no effective credit control policy; as a result, bank credit to the private sector increased by 55 percent in 1970, even though the money supply only increased by 5.6 percent in 1970 and 4.9 percent in 1971.

Faced with continuous deterioration in the balance of payment the government devalued the national currency by 44 percent in 1971 and shifted to liberalization policies. As they occurred in the absence of tighter macroeconomic policies, pressure was put on the trade balance but high world cocoa prices, foreign aid inflows and some debt relief masked this pressure. The government took advantage of high world market prices for cocoa in 1970 to permit a rapid expansion of expenditures and imports, which increased the balance of payments deficit. With accelerating inflation eroding the devaluation of 1967, the real effective exchange rate on imports appreciated at the same time that the import regime was being liberalized. The sharp drop in cocoa prices from US$997 in 1969 to US$565 in 1971 caused the trade account to move into deficit. On December 27, 1971, the currency was devalued by 44 percent.

There was a military coup on 13ᵗʰ January, 1972, so that the administration of the economy changed hands once again from a civilian government to a military government. For the next three years the government embarked on emergency operations without any long-term effort to put the economy on the path of growth and development. The government returned to the controlled regime and increased participation of the state in economic activities. Among the first actions taken by the government was debt repudiation and revaluation of the Cedi by 42 percent, which raised the Cedi from 55 cents to 78 cents (US), so that the extent of the massive devaluation of the Cedi in 1971 was reduced from 44 percent to 26 percent. The coverage of price control was also extended to include other commodities such as motor vehicle components. A new Price and Income Board was created to impose stricter rules on price increases. The government also initiated expansionary fiscal and monetary policy measures. For instance, the expansionary fiscal policy adopted in the 1975 budget at the time when there was a shortfall in government revenues resulted in the government once again resorting to the banking system for the financing of its expenditures. Such financing led to increases in the money supply by 44.6 percent in 1975. To contain aggregate demand, the bank rate was raised from 6 percent to 8.5 percent. However, the average annual increase in the money supply between 1976 and 1978 was well over 50 percent.

A new framework of economic policy was initiated in the form of a Five-Year Development Plan (1975-1980) to formalise and expand the various emergency measures taken by the government since it had taken power. It was another two years before the plan was formally launched. As a result, the budget deficit as a percentage of GDP was higher on average between 1975 and 1978 than under the previous two governments. The fiscal deficit increased from 7.6 percent in 1975 to 11.3 percent in 1976. It fell to 9.5 percent in 1977 and further to 9 percent in 1978. However, the annual growth rate of the money supply increased throughout the period, peaking at 72.4 percent in 1978. To deal with the increasing balance of payment problems, the government devalued the Cedi in 1978 from 1.15 Cedis/US$ at the beginning of the year to 2.75 Cedis/US$.

The political climate between 1978 and 1981 was chaotic with three different governments taking turns to power (two military regimes and one civilian). The macroeconomic environment was equally unstable. All three governments continued the control regime. By the early 1980s, the economic environment was dominated by a general lack of confidence in the economy, both domestically and internationally. Its main causes were the maintenance of fixed and highly overvalued exchange rates that discouraged exports and encouraged imports, as well as expansionary monetary and fiscal policies that led to inflationary pressures and further distorted the real exchange rate. These measures were supplemented by the imposition in 1971 of price controls on all commodities. These discouraged production while providing excessive profits to the unregulated small-scale trading sector. Eventually, the government, in an attempt to stabilize the economy, requested an IMF-supported program.

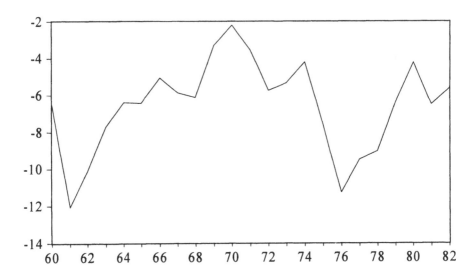

Figure 7.1   Fiscal Deficit to GDP Ratio

Macroeconomic Performance During the Pre-ERP Period (1957-1982)

The overall economic performance over the period 1957-82 proved to be disappointing in many respects. This section discusses the domestic economic performance, while the next section examines the external performance of the economy in the context of the various trade regimes. As reported in Table 7.2, the growth in real GDP immediately after independence was quite impressive. The growth rate of real GDP in 1957 was 4.6 percent and fell to 3.7 percent in 1958. The subsequent two years witnessed a substantial growth of real GDP (15.2 percent in 1959 and 7.5 percent in 1960), due to the massive government expenditure required to achieve the desired industrialization. Between 1961 and 1965, the average growth rate was 3.1 percent. The first negative growth rate of -4.26 percent was registered in 1966, the year of the first military coup.

      The next two governments (the NLC and the civilian government they handed power to) were able to continue the growth performance of the Nkrumah government. The average growth rate from 1967 to 1971 was 5 percent, with the highest growth rate of 9.72 occurring in 1970. The growth performance for the next decade (between 1972 and 1982) was the most disappointing performance since independence, registering a negative average growth rate of -0.95 percent. The growth rate in per capita income also followed the same pattern, a negative average growth rate of -3.4 percent occurring between 1972 and 1982. Specifically, the growth in the per capita income was continuously negative between 1979 and 1982.

Economic performance in terms of inflation followed the pattern of policy regimes, with expansionary fiscal and monetary policies associated with increasing inflation. After inheriting an inflation of 13.2 percent in 1966, the restrictive policies of the NLC government contracted demand enough to register a deflation of 8.4 percent in 1967. However, the devaluation of the Cedi in 1967 finally showed up in the price level via the increased cost of imported goods, so that inflation increased to 7.9 percent and 7.3 percent in 1968 and 1969 respectively.[1]

Inflation performance deteriorated significantly after 1972, with the inflation rate increasing continuously from 10.1 percent in 1972 to 116.5 percent in 1977, a consequence of massive government spending and uncontrolled expansion in the money supply. After a brief fall to 50.1 percent in 1980, it increased again to 116.5 percent in 1981, before falling to 22.3 percent in 1982.

Trade Regimes

Ghana has gone through two cycles of trade and payments regimes since independence in 1957. Each cycle can be defined to consist of the five phases of trade regimes (introduction to the control regime, breakdown of the control system, attempted liberalization, import liberalization, and liberal trade regime), identified by Bhagwati (1978) and Krueger (1978). The first cycle started in 1950 and ended in 1971, while the second cycle runs from 1972 to the present. At independence, Ghana inherited a liberal trade regime, huge external reserves, and a fixed exchange rate system. After experiencing balance of payments problems almost immediately after independence, the government launched a state-led development strategy emphasizing import-substitution industrialization. In addition, in 1961, the government ushered in a controlled regime by introducing exchange controls as a policy package to control and conserve foreign exchange. With the government's refusal in 1961 to accept the IMF/World Bank stabilization package that involved currency devaluation, the exchange controls were extended and an import licence scheme was introduced to solve the increasing balance of payments problems. Throughout the period up to 1966, when a new government took over power, the exchange rate was not adjusted even in the face of sizeable balance of payments deficits. The break down of the control system soon became, especially during 1963 and 1966.

---

[1] The slight decline, despite prudent macroeconomic policies, reflected the devaluation of the Cedi in 1967.

Table 7.2   Macroeconomic Performance Indicators

	Inflation	GDP Per Capita Growth Rates	GDP growth rate
1951	na	na	na
1952	na	na	na
1953	na	na	na
1954	na	na	na
1955	na	na	na
1956	na	na	na
1957	na	na	4.60
1958	na	na	3.70
1959	na	na	15.20
1960	na	na	7.50
1961	na	-1.17	3.43
1962	na	0.63	4.11
1963	na	1.72	4.41
1964	na	0.08	2.21
1965	26.4	-0.46	1.37
1966	13.2	-5.92	-4.26
1967	-8.4	1.25	3.08
1968	7.9	-1.52	0.37
1969	7.3	3.80	6.01
1970	3.0	7.23	9.72
1971	9.6	2.06	5.22
1972	10.1	-5.34	-2.49
1973	17.7	0.00	2.88
1974	18.1	4.07	6.85
1975	29.8	-14.54	-12.43
1976	56.1	-5.62	-3.53
1977	116.5	0.37	2.27
1978	73.1	6.53	8.48
1979	54.4	-4.61	-2.51
1980	50.1	-2.24	0.47
1981	116.5	-6.50	-3.50
1982	22.3	-10.09	-6.92

Sources: IMF: International Financial Statistics;
    World Bank: World Development Indicators.

The military government (NLC) that took power in 1966 and the civilian government they handed over power to pursued more liberal trade policies. As mentioned earlier, the military government put in place an IMF/World Bank-supported stabilization program, which required more restrictive fiscal and monetary policies and removed some of the existing trade controls in an attempt to liberalize the trade regime. In addition, as part of the policies to deal with the increasing balance of payments problems, the government devalued the domestic currency by 43 percent in 1967. The succeeding civilian government implemented further liberalization policies and also devalued the currency by another 44 percent in 1971 to deal with the same balance of payments problems. These devaluations could be taken to mark the end of the first cycle of trade and payments regimes.

The military government that took power in 1972 returned the economy to a control regime by imposing stiffer imports and payments controls. These controls were further stiffened in subsequent years so as to reduce the economy's dependence on external resources. The manufacturing sector of the economy suffered considerably from the import controls. Manufacturing output declined by 5.69 percent in 1974, then increased by 9.25 percent in 1975, only to fall to 4.52 percent in 1976. In response, the government tried to liberalize the economy between 1978 and 1980. These efforts were half-hearted and proved to be unsuccessful since the government hesitated to completely remove the controls, citing balance of payments implications as a reason. In addition, the government refused to devalue the currency. The manufacturing sector output continued to fall by 3.51 percent and 16.84 percent in 1978 and 1979 respectively. Further declines of 19.2 and 20.47 occurred in 1981 and 1982 respectively. Though the decline in the manufacturing sector output between 1974 and 1982 signalled the breakdown of the control regime, the policies continued till early 1983. Unfortunately, the two military coups that led to change in government in 1979 and 1981 on the promise of addressing the economic ills of the country could not restore growth in the manufacturing sector. The nominal exchange rate was kept stable even though the exchange rate was clearly overvalued and eroded the competitiveness of the export sector and even the import substituting one. On these issues, Islam and Wetzel (1994) claimed that rising public sector expenditures were the main cause of the overvaluation of the real exchange rate between 1972 and 1982. Elbadawi and Soto (1995) reported that the real exchange rate was undervalued from 1971 to 1974, and became grossly overvalued thereafter.

Figure 7.2 depicts the evolution of the real exchange rate over the pre-ERP era. The depreciation in the real exchange rate from 1967 to 1972 reflected the devaluations in 1967 and 1971 and the 1972 revaluation. But when domestic inflation started increasing in 1973, the real exchange rate took a sharp turn and appreciated almost continuously till the end of 1982.

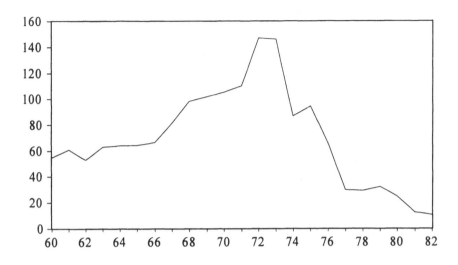

Figure 7.2   Real Exchange Rate (1987=100)

Performance of the External Sector During the Pre-ERP Period (1957-1982)

As a result of the changes in the trade and payments regimes, discussed above, the external sector of the economy witnessed large swings over the pre-ERP era. As Table 7.3 and Figure 7.3 show, on average, the current account balance as a percentage of GDP was negative. This was particularly due to substantial negative balances on the services account, which more than offset any positive trade balance. However, there were some remarkable differences in the current account and balance of payments across various trade and payment regimes. During the controlled regime period of 1961-1966, both the trade balance and current account were on average in deficit, with the current account deficit as a percentage of GDP ranging from -5 percent to -15 percent. The overall balance of payments was also in deficit for about half of the period. The liberalized regime that followed registered positive trade balances from 1967 to 1970 except in 1971 when the trade balance became negative. But the current account deficits carried beyond the control regime up until 1970 when the first current account surplus in more than a decade was achieved. The overall balance of payments also, after registering deficits since 1966, first recorded a surplus in 1970 and continued with surpluses till the government was overthrown in 1972.

Table 7.3   Balance of Payments (Millions of US$)

	Export Value F.O.B	Import Value F.O.B	Trade Balance	Services (net)	Current Account	Overall Balance
1960	333.8	384.1	-14.3	na	-47.9	25.7
1961	332.5	348.7	-52.2	na	-103.5	-21.8
1962	319.9	310.1	9.8	na	-33.7	4.1
1963	307.0	336.6	-29.6	na	-80.1	-40.8
1964	321.4	321.5	-0.1	na	-55.4	-4.2
1965	321.2	439.4	-118.2	na	-222.9	15.2
1966	280.3	320.7	-40.4	na	-127.8	-48.1
1967	284.2	265.4	18.8	na	-84.9	-72.3
1968	304.4	264.4	39.8	na	-56.1	-6.5
1969	345.0	295.3	49.7	na	-60.1	-26.9
1970	427.0	375.1	51.9	na	67.7	25.0
1971	334.6	368.2	-33.6	-112.5	-145.8	34.7
1972	384.3	222.9	161.4	-66.5	108.2	33.1
1973	585.0	372.1	212.9	-98.7	126.3	109.1
1974	679.0	708.2	-29.2	-166.4	-171.5	-142.0
1975	801.0	650.5	150.5	-177.4	17.0	106.3
1976	779.0	690.3	88.7	-189.7	-74.0	-137.3
1977	889.6	860.2	29.4	-167.6	-79.7	-8.5
1978	892.8	780.3	112.5	-189.1	-45.9	-62.3
1979	1065.7	803.1	262.6	-219.4	122.0	69.8
1980	1103.6	908.3	195.3	-245.7	29.2	-1.3
1981	710.7	954.3	-243.6	-260.2	-402.8	-288.3
1982	607.0	588.7	18.3	-209.4	-108.6	-17.9

Sources: IMF: International Financial Statistics;
World Bank: World Development Indicators.

During the next control regime of 1972-1982, a current account surplus was achieved in five out of eleven years, with the last eight years registering relatively small current account deficits or surpluses as a percentage of GDP. The services account during this period was always in deficit, with the size of the deficit in it increasing almost continuously throughout the period. On average, the overall balance of payments was in deficit; however, there were some improvements when compared with the previous regimes. The terms of trade, in general, improved until 1978. The oil price escalation and the decline in the world price of cocoa led to a decline in the terms of trade. By 1982, Ghana had suffered a fall of 59 percent in her terms of trade relative to 1970.

The flow of foreign direct investment (FDI) reflected the economic ideology of the period and the confidence the international community had in the country. For instance during the imports substitution industrialization era of the 1960s capital inflow increased substantially to take advantage of the incentives offered to domestic production of manufactured goods. From a low of 9.9 million dollars in 1962, foreign direct investment increased to 56.1 million dollars in 1966 and to 314.3 million dollars in 1982. There were also some decreases in the external debt, especially between 1972 and 1982. In terms of the total amount, the external debt increased from a low of 571.4 million dollars in 1970 to 1484.2 million dollars in 1982. However, as shown in Figure 7.4, the external debt to GDP ratio decreased almost continuously between 1971 (39.6 percent) and 1982 (4.7 percent), 1966. Due to the military coup in 1966 and its associated uncertainties, FDI decreased continuously for the next three years to reach only 10.2 million dollars in 1969. With a democratically elected government taking power in 1999, FDI increased again to 67.8 million dollars in 1970, but fell to 11.5 million dollars in 1972 when another military government came into power by a military coup. This pattern continued till the end of 1982.

The general trend in the current account and the overall balance of payments led to some large swings in the external reserve position, with decreases in the external debt in some of the years between 1972 and 1982. Table 7.4 summarises the external financial position during the pre-ERP period. Total international reserves decreased almost continuously from 277.9 million dollars in 1960 to 43.1 million dollars in 1971, before increasing again till 1978.

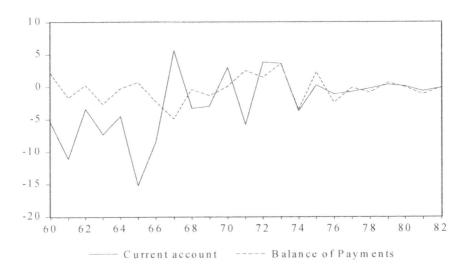

Figure 7.3   Current Account and Balance of Payments (in percent of GDP)

Table 7.4   International Financial Position (millions of US$)

	External Debt	Reserves*	Net Foreign Assets	Foreign Direct Investment
1960	na	277.9	296.0	3.9
1961	na	156.0	170.4	-11.3
1962	na	181.7	153.4	9.9
1963	na	209.3	99.0	7.4
1964	na	125.5	73.9	14.5
1965	na	132.5	-5.7	38.2
1966	na	111.1	-33.5	56.1
1967	na	82.7	-49.5	32.5
1968	na	97.0	-62.3	15.8
1969	na	71.8	-80.5	10.2
1970	571.4	42.6	-19.7	67.8
1971	545.8	43.1	-0.6	30.6
1972	604.4	104.0	99.7	11.5
1973	755.5	194.0	202.0	14.4
1974	758.4	101.3	20.1	10.5
1975	735.0	147.2	127.5	70.9
1976	712.7	113.3	29.3	-18.3
1977	1066.6	181.6	49.2	19.2
1978	1278.6	326.7	105.4	9.7
1979	1282.5	401.2	79.1	-2.8
1980	1401.7	329.6	6.1	15.6
1981	1538.8	268.4	-137.4	16.3
1982	1484.2	314.3	-59.5	16.3

* Includes gold.
Sources: IMF: International Financial Statistics;
World Bank: World Development Indicators.

The flow of foreign direct investment (FDI) reflected the economic ideology of the period and the confidence the international community had in the country. For instance during the imports substitution industrialization era of the 1960s capital inflow increased substantially to take advantage of the incentives offered to domestic production of manufactured goods. From as low as 9.9 million dollars in 1962, foreign direct investment increased to 56.1 million dollars in with 314.3 million dollars in 1982. The increases in the international reserves between 1972 and 1982 were due to the improvements in the overall balance of payments surpluses, discussed earlier. In terms of total amount, the external debt increased from as low as 571.4 million dollars in 1970 to 1484.2 million dollars in 1982. However, as shown in Figure 7.4, the external debt to GDP ratio decreased almost continuously between 1971 (39.6 percent) and 1982 (4.7 percent), 1966. Due to the military coup in 1966 and its associated uncertainties, FDI decreased continuously for the next three years to reach a low of 10.2 million dollars in 1969. With a democratically elected government in power FDI increased again to 67.8 million dollars in 1970, then fell again to 11.5 million dollars in 1972 when another military government came into power by a military coup. This pattern continued till the end of 1982. Net Foreign Assets (NFA) decreased precipitously between 1960 and 1964 and became negative till the end of 1971. This item then became positive in 1972, fluctuated over the next eight years, before becoming negative once again in 1981 and 1982.

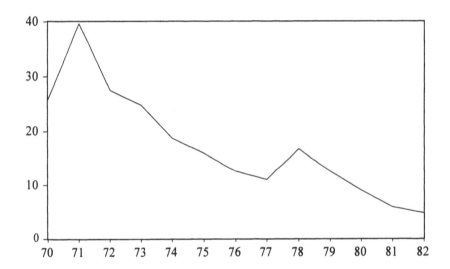

Figure 7.4   External Debt to GDP Ratio

7.2 Economic Policies: Post-ERP Period (1983-2000)

As mentioned earlier, the economic decline worsened by the close of 1982. GDP continued to decline and the inflation rate went into three digits. The rapid and continuous increase in the general price level led to a loss of public confidence in the currency and increased the overvaluation of the Cedi on the foreign exchange markets. In response to the economic problems facing the economy, the government introduced in April 1983 an austerity budget that contained a program of reforms known as the Economic Recovery Program. Fiscal, monetary and exchange rate policies were the main components of the program, which was designed to stimulate domestic aggregate supply by realigning relative prices in favour of the productive sectors. We discuss below the macroeconomic policies adopted in the reform program and their effects on both the domestic and external fronts.

The macroeconomic policies adopted during 1983-2000 to stimulate economic recovery can be divided into two distinct sub-periods. The first sub-period 1983-1991 had a greater commitment to economic stabilization. Inflation was stabilized and the fiscal account registered surpluses continuously for six years. The second period, 1992-2000, with a weakened commitment to stabilization, is associated with extended periods of high and variable inflation, increasing fiscal deficits, excessive growth in the money supply, frequent intense depreciation of the Cedi, falling foreign exchange reserves and excessive foreign debt overhang.

During the first sub-period (1983-1991), the government of Ghana introduced a series of fiscal reforms to stimulate economic recovery. The reforms focused on controlling the rate of growth of government expenditures, increasing government revenues and reducing the size of the deficit on current accounts, thereby reducing government recourse to the banking system to finance deficit. Tax revenue as a percentage of GDP increased from a low level of 5.6 percent in 1983 to 14.4 percent in 1986 and further increased to 15.2 percent by 1991. These increases were mainly due to the new measures adopted to improve the tax collection machinery and administration, as well as general improvement in the economy. Due to the confidence engendered by the ERP, foreign grants became an important part of government revenue. Available figures show a rising trend of foreign grants as a percentage of total government revenue from 4.01 percent in 1985 to 9.94 percent in 1989. Some discipline was also introduced into government expenditures. While government total expenditures as a percentage of GDP increased from 8.2 percent in 1983 to 14 percent in 1985, they remained almost constant from 1985 to 1991. The overall budget deficit/surplus as a percentage of GDP improved from a deficit of 2.7 percent in 1983 to surpluses of 0.54 percent in 1987, 0.73 percent in 1989 and then to 1.6 percent by 1991. Consequently, government's recourse to the banking sector to finance its budget deficits was substantially reduced (refer to Figure 7.5 for the evolution of the budget deficit/surplus to the GDP ratio). Under the Economic Recovery Program that was put in place in 1983, Ghana replaced a fixed exchange rate regime with that of flexible determination of the exchange rate. In the gradual switch to a flexible exchange rate regime, there were several devaluations between 1983 and 1986. A foreign exchange auction was introduced in 1986. The foreign exchange bureau was set up in 1988 and an interbank market was established in 1992.

Due to the expansion of credit to the private sector, growth in money supply accelerated between 1983 and 1989, with an average rate of 49 percent. Though there were some controls on credit to the private sector, there were still some substantial increases of credit to that sector. In percentages, the annual increase in total bank credit to the private sector rose from 15.5 percent in 1986 to 34.4 percent in 1990.

Economic policies took a sharp turn in 1992. Related to national elections to usher in a civilian government in 1992, there were substantial increases in government expenditures. The fiscal budget registered a deficit of 5.2 percent of GDP in 1992. With the exception of some improvements in 1994 and 1995 when the budget registered surpluses of 2.1 percent and 0.9 percent of GDP respectively, all other years after 1992 recorded deficits in the government budget. Growth in the money supply touched an all time high of 66 percent in 1992 and stayed relatively high till the end of 2000 when it was reduced to 38.2 percent. This was associated with the appreciation of the real exchange rate, with adverse consequences for exports.

Table 7.5   Macroeconomic Policy Indicators

	Growth in money	Budget Deficit*	Deficit to GDP ratio	Exchange Rate	Grants to GDP ratio
1983	49.2	-4933.3	-2.7	30.0	0.03
1984	60.6	-4843	-1.8	50.0	0.34
1985	42.7	-7579	-2.2	60.0	0.47
1986	44.0	299	0.1	90.0	0.76
1987	52.6	4059	0.5	176.1	0.81
1988	45.0	3911	0.4	229.9	1.10
1989	52.7	10300	0.7	303.0	1.50
1990	10.8	3300	0.2	344.8	1.37
1991	7.7	39000	1.6	390.6	1.50
1992	53.0	-144400	-5.2	520.8	1.17
1993	27.9	-97300	-2.5	819.7	1.72
1994	50.3	111700	2.1	1052.6	0.76
1995	33.4	70300	0.9	1449.3	1.21
1996	31.7	-335500	-3.0	1754.4	0.68
1997	46.0	-297600	-2.1	2272.7	0.47
1998	20.9	-1048800	-2.5	2325.6	na
1999	15.8	na	na	3535.1	na
2000	38.2	na	na	7047.7	na

* In millions of Ghanaian Cedis.
Sources: IMF: International Financial Statistics;
        World Bank: World Development Indicators.

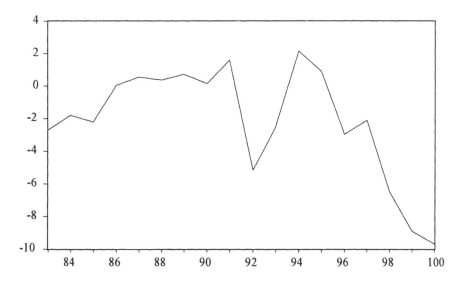

Figure 7.5   Fiscal Deficit to GDP Ratio

Macroeconomic Performance

The result of the stabilization program under ERP was immediate and positive during the first half of the post-ERP period. In 1984 the economy registered significant improvement, as shown by the growth rates in Table 7.5 below. Real GDP rose by 8.6 percent and the per capita real income recorded a commendable growth of 4.6 percent. These remarkable improvements continued up to the end of 1989 with GDP growth of 5.1 percent and GDP per capita growth of 2.4 percent. With a brief decline in the economy in 1990, growth picked up again in 1991. Growth at the sectoral level varied more widely. Services showed rapid and consistent growth averaging about 7.1 percent between 1984 and 1991. The growth performance in the industrial sector was also impressive between 1984 and 1992, with a growth rate of 17.6 percent in 1985. Though the growth momentum slowed in 1986 to a growth rate of 7.6 percent, it picked up again in 1987 (11.5 percent) and 1988 (11.4 percent). It then settled for an average annual rate of 4.8 percent between 1989 and 1992. The performance of the agriculture sector slowed and varied the most during the first half of the post-ERP period. The sector recorded 9.7 percent in 1984, only to achieve 0.7 percent in the next year. In 1990 agricultural output declined by 2 percent, picked up again in 1991 with a 4.7 percent growth rate, only to suffer another decline by 0.6 percent in 1992. However, the overall strong improvement in GDP growth and demand management led to a reduction of inflation: the inflation rate declined precipitously from 122.8 percent in 1983 to 25.2 percent in 1989. By 1992, inflation had been brought down to 10 percent.

Table 7.6   Macroeconomic Policy Indicators

	Inflation	GDP Per Capita Growth Rates	GDP growth rate
1983	122.9	-8.02	-4.56
1984	39.7	4.58	8.65
1985	10.3	1.14	5.09
1986	24.6	1.56	5.20
1987	39.8	1.48	4.79
1988	31.4	2.62	5.63
1989	25.2	2.40	5.09
1990	37.3	1.00	3.33
1991	18.0	2.76	5.28
1992	10.1	1.23	3.88
1993	25.0	2.02	4.85
1994	24.9	0.37	3.30
1995	60.0	1.01	4.11
1996	46.6	1.74	4.60
1997	27.9	1.62	4.20
1998	14.6	2.38	4.70
1999	12.4	2.35	4.41
2000	25.2	1.92	3.70

Sources: IMF: International Financial Statistics;
World Bank: World Development Indicators.

The change in the policy direction in 1992 affected the performance of the economy in terms of both growth and inflation. The increases in government spending combined with increases in the money supply eventually led to a rise in inflation. Inflation increased to 25 percent in 1993 and to 60 percent in 1995, even though there were budget surpluses in 1994 and 1995. Though inflation was briefly brought under control to the level of 12.4 percent in 1999, it increased again to 25.2 percent in 2000. After 1992, growth rates in GDP and per capita GDP were also unimpressive when compared with their performances up to 1991. Sectoral growth performances were mixed. Growth in the services sector remained impressive, averaging about 5.8 percent between 1992 and 2000. The agriculture and the industrial sectors experienced the most volatile growth performance.

Trade Regimes and Exchange Rate Policies

The post-ERP period has seen three different trade and payments regimes in Ghana. These are the attempted liberalization regime of 1983-86; the import liberalization regime of 1987-89; and the liberal trade regime of 1990-2000. The changes in the exchange rate policies were among the most important measures adopted during the three trade regimes. The attempted liberalization regime, which began in April 1983 and lasted till 1986, saw four nominal devaluations of the Ghanaian Cedi (see Table 7.4) and represented the transition from the fixed exchange rate system to a liberalized exchange rate one. The government introduced in April 1983 a scheme of surcharges and bonuses that effectively created a multiple exchange rate system. In the same year, the government initiated an import liberalization process as part of its broad macroeconomic program, the objective of which was to eliminate the negative effects of the preceding extremely restrictive control regime. However, the import licensing system that the government inherited from the preceding government was maintained until 1986. A foreign exchange retail auction was introduced in September 1986, which eventually culminated in the official introduction of a two-tier system under which imports and exports of selected goods were subject to the official exchange rate while all other transactions were subject to the weekly auction rate. The structure of taxes on foreign trade virtually remained the same between 1983 and 1985. However, in 1986, an escalating tariff structure was established with raw materials and capital goods imports facing a lower import tariff rate than consumer finished goods imports.

In 1987 the government began the elimination of the import licensing system by replacing quotas and other restrictions with tariffs. The fixed exchange rate system was also brought to a conclusion and a new era of flexible exchange system was ushered in. The tax schedules on foreign trade were also adjusted upwards in 1987 but were eventually reduced in 1988 to levels lower than what they were in 1986. However, the escalating tariff structure was maintained. There was also significant relaxation of the exchange control regulations. The two-tier exchange rate system between 1986 and 1988 could not eliminate the considerable and growing spread between the parallel and official exchange rates. In February 1988, the parallel market was legalized with the establishment of the foreign exchange bureaux. As a result of the liberalization of the trade and payment regimes, the spread of about 40 percent between the foreign bureaux buying rates and the Bank of Ghana auction rate at the beginning of 1989 was narrowed to less than 10 percent within the year.

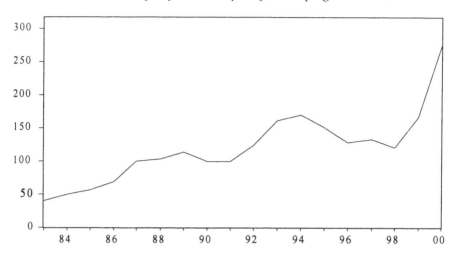

Figure 7.6   Real Exchange Rates (1987=100), Post-ERP Period

In January 1989, the import licensing system was completely removed, since the liberalization of the foreign exchange market no longer supported the import licensing system. The tax schedules on foreign trade were continuously reduced till the end of 2000. Among further efforts to liberalize the exchange rate system, the government introduced the wholesale auction system in 1990. This was later replaced by the interbank exchange market system in 1992. This system continued to 2000.

The evolution of the real exchange rate over the post-ERP period is shown in Figure 7.6 below. The real exchange rate depreciated almost continuously throughout the post-ERP period, with the steepest depreciation occurring between 1998 and 2000. These depreciations were mostly caused by the rapid depreciation of the nominal exchange rate. For example, the steep real depreciation of the Ghanaian Cedi between 1998 and 2000 was mainly caused by a 203 percent nominal depreciation over the same period.

Performance of the External Sector

The current account balance during the entire post-ERP period has been in deficit. This is mainly due to the liberalization process, including the gradual elimination of import restrictions as the economy moved towards a more liberal trade regime. Another important cause of the deficit is the almost continuous decline in the terms of trade after 1984, so that the trade balance deficits were mainly due to increases in imports values and decline in export values. The fall in the price of cocoa by almost 50 percent between 1987 and 1989 led to a loss of cocoa revenue of US$200 million in 1989, though cocoa exports nearly doubled in volume. Table 7.6 and Figure 7.7 show the developments in the balance of payments during the period. The current account was in deficit for the whole period. As a percentage of GDP, the current account deteriorated continuously from a low of 4 percent in 1983 to 22.7 percent in 1993, just a year after the commitment to the economic recovery program took a sharp turn. Thereafter, it varied around an average of 13 percent and closed the period with 10 percent. The overall balance of payment performed very well due to the increased confidence the international financial community had in the recovery program, thereby leading to increases in capital inflows. These inflows overshadowed the worsening current account, allowing significant balance of payments surpluses. For instance, between 1987 and 1998 (except in 1992 and 1996), the balance of payments recorded surpluses. It is no surprise that these balance of payments deficits occurred in election years when the trade and current account deficits increased significantly, at the time when the international financial community were pessimistic about the direction of the economy.

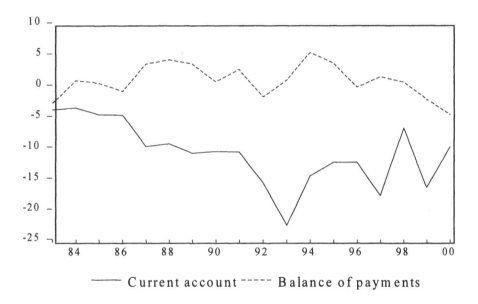

Figure 7.7 Current Account and Balance of Payments (in percent of GDP)

Table 7.7   International Financial Position (millions US$)

	External Debt	Reserves	Net Foreign Assets*	Foreign Direct Investment
1983	1665.9	291.3	-244.4	2.4
1984	1959.4	437.2	-404.8	2.0
1985	2246.9	552.1	-598.7	5.6
1986	2754.5	624.0	-660.2	4.3
1987	3296.7	331.6	-773.1	4.7
1988	3084.3	310.3	-754.2	5.0
1989	3361.4	435.9	-787.7	15.0
1990	3837.1	309.3	-681.5	14.8
1991	4333.2	644.3	53.8	20.0
1992	4460.1	411.6	-148.0	22.5
1993	4833.6	517.0	-52.2	125.0
1994	5415.9	689.3	206.3	233.0
1995	5888.0	803.8	344.0	106.5
1996	6402.2	930.3	419.7	120.0
1997	6313.1	617.6	431.8	82.6
1998	6933.1	456.7	459.6	167.4
1999	6979.3	534.8	94.1	243.7
2000	6624.9	308.9	-1.3	165.9

* Includes gold.
Sources: IMF: International Financial Statistics;
             World Bank: World Development Indicators.

Besides the improvements in the balance of payments, Table 7.7 shows that total international reserves continued to experience large swings during the post-ERP period. In millions of US dollars, they increased from 291.3 in 1983 to 624 in 1986, decreased to 310.3 in 1988 and then increased again to 930.3 by 1996. they finally fell to 308.9 million dollars in 2000. The movements in foreign direct investment indicate that foreign investors were initially cautiously optimistic about the success of the economic recovery program. For almost four years after the implementation of the stabilization programme, foreign direct investments only increased from 2.4 million dollars in 1984 to 4.7 million dollars in 1987. Once they were confident about the direction of the economy, foreign direct investment increased substantially, reaching 233 million dollars in 1994. By 2000, foreign direct investment was about 166 million dollars.

In addition to encouraging inflows of loans from official sources and foreign direct investment, the stabilization and liberalization programs also encouraged the inflow of private transfers by Ghanaians resident abroad. Between 1983 and 1987, private transfers increased by more than 30 times (from $US 4.02 million in 1983 to $US 122.4 million in 1987). The increases continued up to 2000. Due to increases in official and bilateral capital inflows, total external debt increased continuously from 1983 to 1999, before decreasing marginally in 2000. As shown in Figure 7.8, total external debt as a percentage of GDP trended upwards from a low of 27 percent in 1983 to 172 percent in 2000.

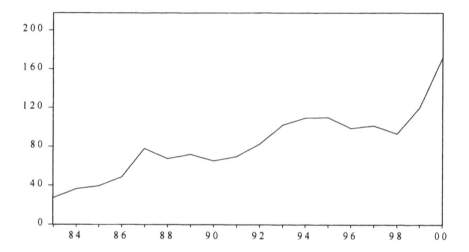

Figure 7.8 External Debt to GDP Ratio

Conclusions

This chapter identified the political environment and its associated economic policy regimes for the Ghanaian economy, as well as its economic performance. The Ghanaian macroeconomic experience from its independence in 1957 to 1982 is almost a classic example of that of many developing nations during similar periods. Immediately after independence, Ghana basically pursued an inward looking strategy with the objective of fostering self-sufficiency. This strategy initiated industrialization efforts aimed at import substitution, but also led to massive government spending, which caused increases in budget and current account deficits. Monetization of the budget deficits to a considerable extent led to inflation. Subsequent governments after the first republic (1957-66) attempted a development strategy led by the private sector, but with little success. Though there was some improvement in the current account balance, the budget deficits and the problems caused by them persisted. The growth performance varied according to the policy regimes: the controlled regimes were associated with a slowdown of real GDP growth while the liberal economic regimes registered higher growth rates.

The major reorientation of macroeconomic policy took place in 1983 when the government introduced an IMF sponsored Economic Recovery Program. The restrictive fiscal and monetary policies that were implemented during it brought down inflation and improved the fiscal balances for the next eight years. However, government expenditures were increased substantially in 1992 and economic policies took a sharp turn towards a more expansionary stance. With the exception of a few years, inflation increased and fiscal balances deteriorated. The current account of the balance of payments deteriorated even though a flexible exchange rate policy was implemented. The rising inflation led to a real depreciation of the Ghanaian Cedi.

As part of the overall policy regime, trade and payments arrangements swung from liberal to highly controlled ones especially during the pre-ERP era. Significant liberalisation was attempted during the post-ERP period. Exchange rate policies have also differed according to the trade regime, with fixed rates accompanying the control regimes and flexible exchange rates system constituting an integral element of the liberal regimes. There appears to have been a distinct association between trade regimes and current account position: in general, current account balances as a percentage of GDP tended to improve during the control regime and deteriorated during the liberal regime. This association clearly requires an empirical study to identify the true relationship between macroeconomic policies and the external performance of the Ghanaian economy while paying particular attention to the role played by changes in the exchange rate. The next chapter conducts such an empirical study based on the intertemporal approach to the current account, as done in earlier chapters for analysing Nigeria's current account.

Chapter 8

Econometric Analysis of
Ghana's Current Account

Introduction

The preceding chapter discussed the nature of domestic macroeconomic policies and their effects on the external sector of the Ghanaian economy for the period from 1960 to 2000. The recurring pattern that emerged was that anytime there was a change in the trade regime and macroeconomic stance, the performance of the external economy was affected very significantly. This chapter reports the econometric analysis of Ghana's current account based on the present value model of the current account (PVMCA). The theoretical and econometric basis of this analysis was laid out in earlier chapters and has already been applied to the Nigerian economy. This chapter tests the basic model and the various extensions of the PVMCA specified in Chapter 4.

This chapter is organized as follows. Section 8.1 discusses the data and derivation of the variables used for the empirical analysis. Section 8.2 tests the standard present value model of the current account (the benchmark PVMCA). Section 8.3 conducts empirical tests to determine the extent to which external shocks can affect a country's current balances. This section uses an extended version of the benchmark PVMCA to include changes in the interest and exchange rates. Section 8.4 presents the results obtained from extending the PVMCA further to include changes in the terms of trade. Section 8.5 presents the results of a further extension of the PVMCA to account for possible asymmetry in the access to the international financial sector.

8.1 Data and Parameter Values

The empirical analysis of this chapter is based on annual data for the period 1960-1997. The data was obtained from the International Financial Statistics (IFS). The data on private consumption, government spending, investment and gross domestic product (GDP) were converted to real per capita by dividing the nominal variables by the GDP deflator (1995=100) and the level of total population. The net output variable (Q_t) was constructed by subtracting investment and government spending from GDP. The series for the current account (ca_t) of the balance of payments was constructed by subtracting the sum of consumption, investment and government spending from GDP. To obtain the change in the net output series (ΔQ_t), we took the log and first difference of the net output series.

We used the London Interbank Offer Rate (LIBOR), adjusted for expected inflation in the industrial countries, to proxy for the world real interest rate (r_t). Given that the available real exchange rate data for Ghana from the IFS starts from 1975, we computed a proxy series in the following manner. We first computed the bilateral exchange rates between Ghana and her six largest trading partners (United Kingdom, Germany, USA, Japan, France and the Netherlands). Then we constructed the weighted real exchange rate index for each country using the calculated nominal exchange rates and the consumer price indices for Ghana and the relevant trading partner (1995=100). The weight assigned to a trading partner is based on the extent of trade flows between Ghana and the relevant trading partner. The terms of trade is defined as the relative price of imports in terms of exports. The *ex-ante* expected change in the exchange rate and the terms of trade are computed using a one-year autoregression. The data for the empirical analysis are provided in Appendix II. To compute the first set of the consumption-based interest rates, $\hat{r}$, we adjusted the world interest rate for the expected change in the exchange rate. The second set of the consumption-based interest rate, $\hat{\hat{r}}$, was computed by adjusting the world real interest rate for a change in both the real exchange rate and the terms of trade. The procedures for these adjustments were specified in Chapter 4.

The test for the optimal current account derived from the PVMCA and expressed in equations (4.58), (4.67), and (4.74) of Chapter 4 requires the use of other parameters such as the intertemporal substitution variable γ, the share of tradable/importable goods in the total consumption α, and the preference parameter β. For consistency with our study on Nigeria, we again adopt values used by other studies. Following Ostry and Reinhart (1992), we use 0.45 for the intertemporal substitution variable γ, and 0.85 for the share α of tradable goods in total consumption. Using the sample mean of the series on LIBOR, we calculated the preference parameter to be 0.97.

8.2 Test of the Benchmark PVMCA Model for Ghana

The equation describing the optimal current account for the benchmark PVMCA was derived in Chapter 4 and was labelled as equation (4.33). For convenience at this stage, it is restated below as equation (8.1).

$$CA^* = -[1\ 0](1+r^*)^{-1}\Psi(1-(1+r^*)^{-1}\Psi)^{-1}\begin{bmatrix}\Delta Q_t\\CA_t\end{bmatrix}$$

$$= [\Phi_{\Delta Q}\ \Phi_{CA}]\begin{bmatrix}\Delta Q_t\\CA_t\end{bmatrix} \tag{8.1}$$

where Ψ is the vector autoregression (VAR) parameters, CA* is the optimal current account, ΔQ_t is change in net output and $r*$ is the world interest rate, which is proxied by the London Interbank Offer Rate (LIBOR). Equation (8.1) does not include changes in the interest rate, exchange rate or the terms of trade. It simply shows how the current account responds to temporal changes in net output, thereby serving the role that savings play when households smooth consumption. It embodies the basic idea that a country will only run a current account deficit if it expects its net output to rise in the future. The country will run a surplus if it expects its net output to fall in the future. The testable implications of equation (8.1) are as follows: the variables included in the VAR are stationary, the optimal current account is stationary, the variance of the actual current account and the optimal/predicted current account are equal, and that $[\Phi_{\Delta Q} \, \Phi_{CA}] = [1 \; 0]$.

To test for the stationarity of the variables entering the VAR, we conducted the Augmented Dickey-Fuller (ADF) and the Phillips-Perron (VAR) tests. Table 8.1 presents the results for these tests without a constant and a time trend, since the variables are expressed as deviations from their means. Both variables included in the VAR are found to be stationary at the 5 percent significance levels (the 5 percent critical value of both tests and for the two variables is −1.95). According to the theory, the optimal current account must also be stationary since it must be the same as the actual current account. The ADF and the PP tests indicate that the optimal current account is also stationary at the 5 percent significance level.[1]

In order to test for the $[\Phi_{\Delta Q} \, \Phi_{CA}] = [1 \; 0]$ restriction of equation (8.1), we need to estimate a VAR in ΔQ and CA. Table 8.2 reports the VAR equations estimated by OLS.

Table 8.1   Unit Root Tests

Variables	ADF*	PP*
Change in net output	-4.57	-5.12
Actual current account	-5.03	-5.29
Optimal current account	-4.31	-7.61

* ADF indicates the Augmented Dickey-Fuller test; PP represents the Phillips-Perron test.

---

[1] The lag length of one for this VAR and all others was chosen using the Akaike Information Criterion and the Schwartz Criterion.

Table 8.2   VAR Estimates

Equation	Regressors	
	ΔQ_{t-1}	CA_{t-1}
ΔQ_t	0.113	-0.021
	(0.166)	(0.122)
CA_t	-0.081	0.824
	(0.129)	(0.095)

Standard errors are in parentheses.

Table 8.3   Test of the Benchmark Model

ΔQ_t	-0.115
	(0.112)
CA_t	0.252
	(0.185)

$\chi^2 = 305.32$; p-value = 0.000; var(CA^*)/var(CA) = 0.26
Standard errors are in parentheses.

The Akaike Information Criterion (AIC) and the Schwartz Criterion (SC) was used to select the optimal lag, which proved to be one. The result of the test of the benchmark model is presented in Table 8.3. The estimated values of $[\Phi_{\Delta Q} \; \Phi_{CA}]$ are [-0.11 0.25]. The coefficients on both the current account and net output are not significantly different from zero. This constitutes a rejection of the benchmark model. The χ^2 of the Wald test of the parameter restrictions on the VAR also rejects the model with a p-value of zero. The ratio (in Table 8.3) of the variance of the optimal current account to that of the actual current account also indicates that the variance of the predicted current account is only 26 percent of the actual current account. This indicates that other factors that might have influenced the current account were not captured by the benchmark PVMCA. Consistent with the results from the Wald test, Figure 8.1 shows that the benchmark PVMCA model does not provide a satisfactory fit for the actual current account data, though it does seem to perform relatively much better in capturing the increasing deficits from the late 1980s until the end of the data period.

The strong rejection of the benchmark PVMCA model seems to indicate that it fails to capture some factors that were important in the determination of

Ghana's current account during the period under study. This finding is consistent with our conclusion in Chapter 7 that shifts in the trade and exchange regimes in Ghana were instrumental in determining the general direction of the current account. We next attempt to capture these effects by extending the benchmark PVMCA model to include other important variables, namely changes in the world interest rate, exchange rate and the terms of trade.

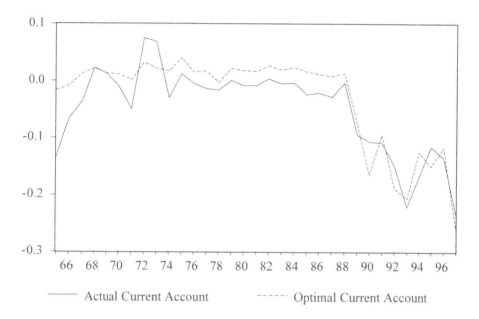

—— Actual Current Account   ------ Optimal Current Account

Figure 8.1   Actual and Optimal Current Account

8.3 Extending the Benchmark Model to Include External Shocks

Chapter 4 extended the benchmark PVMCA model to incorporate changes in the world interest rate, the exchange rate and the terms of trade (measured as the relative price of importables). These extensions are necessary for a small open economy for the following important reasons. First, external shocks could affect the economy and its external sector significantly. For instance, as individuals adjust their saving behaviour to respond to changes in the real interest rate, the country may also adjust its current account in response to changes in the world interest rate. Bergin and Sheffrin (2000) argued that the exclusion of external shocks from the benchmark PVMCA model could explain why the model has often been rejected by studies that use data from small open economies. In addition, if we relax the assumption of one tradable good in the benchmark model to include nontradable goods, then changes in the real exchange rate measured as the relative price of tradable goods can impact on the current account. This effect was confirmed earlier in this book for Nigeria's current account. It seems likely that changes in Ghana's terms of trade will also exert a significant effect on its current account balances, especially since it depends on a few agriculture products for its foreign exchange earnings. We, therefore, proceed to test for Ghana the extended versions of the PVMCA specified in Chapter 4. To do so, we first test the extension of the model to capture changes in the world interest rate and the exchange rate. Later, we extend the model further to include changes in the terms of trade.

8.3 PVMCA Incorporating Changes in the Exchange Rate and the World Interest Rate

If we extend the model to capture changes in the world interest rate and the exchange rate, the equation describing the optimal current account balances is given by:

$$hz_t = -\sum_{t=T+1}^{\infty} \beta^{t-T} (g_1 - g_2)^{t-T} z_t \qquad (8.2)$$

where $z_t = (\Delta Q_t, CA_t, \hat{r})'$, $g_1 = [1\ 0\ 0]$, $g_2 = [0\ 0\ 1]$, $h = [0\ 1\ 0]$, and $\hat{r}$ is the consumption-based interest rate derived from the world real interest rate and expected changes in the exchange rate. As shown in equation (4.59) of Chapter 4, the right hand side of equation (8.2) can be re-written as:

$$CA_t^{**} = k\ z_t \qquad (8.3)$$

where $k = -(g_1 - g_2)\beta\psi\ (I - \beta\psi)^{-1}$.

To obtain the consumption-based interest rate as defined in equation (4.45) of Chapter 4, we again used 0.45 for the intertemporal elasticity and 0.85 for the share of tradable goods. The justification for using these values was given in Chapter 4.

For testing equation (8.2), we need to ensure that the variables entering the VAR process are stationary. Table 8.4 summarizes the results of the Augmented Dickey-Fuller (ADF) and Phillips-Perron (PP) unit root tests. These results indicate that all of the variables entering the VAR are stationary at the 5 percent significant level. According to equation (5.1) of Chapter 5, if the change in net output and the actual current account are stationary, then the optimal account must also be stationary. This is confirmed for the Ghanaian data by the ADF and the PP tests, which indicate that the optimal current account is stationary at the 5 percent significance level.

The VAR parameters used in calculating the optimal current account are reported in Table 8.5. We chose one lag length using the Akaike Information

Criterion and the Schwartz Criterion. The present value test results reported in Table 8.6 show a significant improvement over the corresponding ones for the benchmark PVMCA model. With the introduction of changes in the world interest rate and the exchange rate, the extended PVMCA's prediction is fairly consistent with the theory: the estimates of the k-vector are [-0.63 1.12 0.09], which is close to the theoretically expected value [0 1 0] except for the coefficient on the change in net output. The coefficient on the change in net output (-0.63) is greater than its theoretical value of zero though the coefficients on the current account and the consumption-based interest rate are close to their theoretical values. The reported χ^2 statistics and its p-value indicate that the model extended to include changes in the consumption-based interest rate cannot be rejected. This lends support to the idea advanced in Chapter 7 that the various trade regimes in Ghana and their associated exchange rate policies affected current account balances over the period under study. In comparison with the benchmark model, the volatility of the predicted current account is improved in terms of being closer to the variability in the actual current account. However, the variability in the predicted current account exceeds that of the actual by 14 percent. The greater volatility of the optimal current account relative to the actual one suggests the absence of speculation as the driving force behind capital movements. In addition, it implies that economic agents do not have full access to the international financial markets.

Figure 8.2 shows that the optimal current account incorporating changes in the consumption-based interest rate tracks the actual current account relatively closely, when compared with that derived from the benchmark PVMCA model. Therefore, both Table 8.5 and Figure 8.2 confirm that the current account of Ghana is affected by changes in the world interest rate and the exchange rate in addition to shocks to output, government expenditure, and investment expenditure. Chapter 4 had reached a similar conclusion for Nigeria. Therefore, we conclude that since both Nigeria and Ghana are small open economies, the current account of such economies, in general, is likely to be affected by changes in the world interest rate and the exchange rate in addition to shocks to output, government expenditures, and investment expenditures.

Table 8.4   Unit Root Tests

Variables	ADF*	PP*
Change in net output	-4.57	-5.12
Actual current account	-5.03	-5.29
Optimal current account	-3.01	-3.51
Consumption-based Interest rate	-4.16	-5.29

* ADF indicates the Augmented Dickey-Fuller test; PP represents the Phillips-Perron test.

Table 8.5   VAR Estimates

	Regressors		
Equation	ΔQ_{t-1}	CA_{t-1}	$\hat{r}_{t-1}$
ΔQ_t	0.101	-0.001	-0.018
	(0.181)	(0.139)	(0.025)
CA_t	-0.113	0.859	0.023
	(0.134)	(0.104)	(0.026)
$\hat{r}_t$	-0.822	0.457	0.081
	(1.242)	(0.962)	(0.177)

Standard errors are in parentheses.

A policy implication that can be drawn from the above findings is the following. For the greater part of the period under study, the Ghanaian government pursued trade and payment policies that introduced strict capital controls and kept the exchange rate fixed. The economy, therefore, missed the opportunity of using the exchange rate and changes in the world interest rate to improve its current account balances.

8.4 The PVMCA Incorporating Changes in the Terms of Trade, Interest Rates and Exchange Rates

We next test the version of the extended PVMCA incorporating changes in the terms of trade along with changes in the world interest rate and the exchange rate. The equation describing the optimal current account balances in this case is now given by:

$$hz_t = - \sum_{t=T+1}^{\infty} \beta^{t-T} (g_1 - g_2)^{t-T} z_t \qquad (8.4)$$

where $z_t = (\Delta Q_t, CA_t, \hat{r})'$, $g_1 = [1\ 0\ 0]$, $g_2 = [0\ 0\ 1]$ $h = [0\ 1\ 0]$, and $\hat{r}$ is the consumption-based interest rate incorporating the world real interest rate, expected changes in the exchange rate and the terms of trade. Again, as shown for equation (4.59) of Chapter 4, for given z_t, the right hand side of equation (8.4) can be rewritten as:

$$CA_t^{**} = k\, z_t \qquad (8.5)$$

where $k = - (g_1 - g_2)\beta\psi\, (I - \beta\psi)^{-1}$.

Table 8.6   Test of the Extended PVMCA (Including Changes in the Interest Rate and Exchange Rate)

ΔQ_t	-0.636
	(0.537)
CA	1.123
	(0.053)
$\hat{r}_t$	0.093
	(0.078)

$\chi^2 = 2.32$; p-value = 0.247; var(CA*)/var(CA)= 1.14

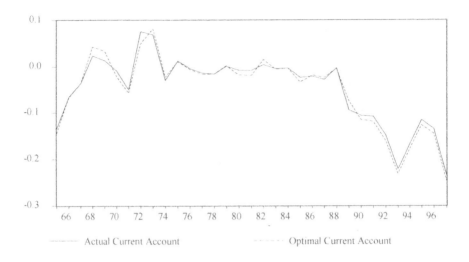

------- Actual Current Account   ------- Optimal Current Account

Figure 8.2   Actual and Optimal Current Account

To obtain the consumption-based interest rate for equation (4.45) of Chapter 4, with $\hat{\hat{r}}$ replacing $\hat{r}$, we used the value 0.45 for the intertemporal elasticity and the value 0.85 for the share of tradable goods. To perform tests for equation (8.4), the variables entering the VAR process have to be stationary. Table 8.7 summarises the results of the ADF and PP tests. These indicate that all variables entering the VAR are stationary. All reported test statistics are greater than the critical value of 1.95 for both tests. Also, the optimal current account is stationary at the 5 percent significance level, confirming the theoretical expectation of stationarity of the optimal current account asserted by equation (5.1). The Akaike Information Criterion and the Schwartz Criterion indicated that the optimal lag was one. The results from the one lag VAR are reported in Table 8.8.

The estimate of the k vector reported in Table 8.9 is [0.21 0.25 -0.02]. The estimates are significantly different from their theoretical expected values of [0 1 0], except for the coefficient (-0.02) on the consumption-based interest rate (adjusted for expected changes in the exchange rate and terms of trade). The coefficient (0.21) on the change in net output is greater than its theoretical value of zero, but is not significantly different from zero. The coefficient (0.25) of the current account is very much less than its theoretical value of one. The reported χ^2 statistic and its p-value indicate a rejection of this extension of the PVMCA model (i.e., incorporating changes in the consumption-based interest rate that includes expected changes in both the exchange rate and the terms of trade). A possible explanation for this disappointing result is that the terms of trade are one of the major determinants of the real exchange rate for Ghana, so that adding the terms of trade to a model that already includes the real exchange rate is not expected to lead to a significant improvement. Further, including the terms of trade in the model may have over-accounted for the external shocks to the current account. This may be the reason for the poor performance of this version of the model. As shown in Table 8.9, the volatility of the predicted current account is only 13 percent of that of the actual current account. The χ^2 of the Wald test of the parameter restrictions on the VAR also rejects the model with a p-value of zero.

Figure 8.3 shows that the optimal current account based on changes in the consumption-based interest rate and incorporating changes in the expected exchange rate and terms of trade does not perform well. Though it seems to track the actual current account during the pre-ERP period, it diverges significantly from the current account for the ERP era.

8.5 Asymmetry in Access to the International Financial Market

The government of Ghana has from time to time attempted to manage the international mobility of capital with measures of capital controls as part of the overall trade regime. As discussed in Chapter 7, the period prior to 1983 (with the exception of the period 1969 to 1972) had various forms of exchange controls to complement the overall control regime followed by various governments. These restrictions prevented economic agents in the Ghanaian economy from having full access to the international financial markets. Further, the political and macroeconomic sources of instability in the Ghanaian economy reduced the growth potential of the economy and the ability of private agents to pay back funds borrowed on the international financial markets. In such a context, the international financial markets are likely to be reluctant to lend to Ghanaians who want to smooth their consumption, even though the Ghanaians often seem to have managed to find ways to send their excess funds abroad. This suggests that there may have been asymmetrical access to the international financial market and the need to test this hypothesis for economic agents in Ghana.

Table 8.7   Unit Root Tests

Variables	ADF*	PP*
Change in net output	-4.57	-5.12
Actual current account	-5.03	-5.29
Optimal current account	-3.91	-3.64
Consumption-based Interest rate	-5.63	-7.86

* ADF refers to the Augmented Dickey-Fuller test; PP refers to the Phillips-Perron test.

Table 8.8   VAR Estimates

	Regressors		
Equation	ΔQ_{t-1}	CA_{t-1}	$\hat{r}_{t-1}$
ΔQ_t	0.071	-0.061	0.478
	(0.182)	(0.133)	(0.688)
CA_t	-0.001	0.861	-0.027
	(0.139)	(0.101)	(0.526)
$\hat{r}_t$	-0.034	0.061	-0.232
	(0.045)	(0.032)	(0.171)

Standard errors are in parentheses.

Table 8.9   Test of the Modified PVMCA (Incorporating Changes in the Interest Rate, Exchange Rate and Terms of Trade)

ΔQ_t	0.213
	(0.742)
CA	0.250
	(0.121)
$\hat{\hat{r}}_t$	-0.022
	(0.136)

$\chi^2 = 267.35$; p-value = 0.000; var(CA*)/var(CA)= 0.13
Standard errors are in parentheses.

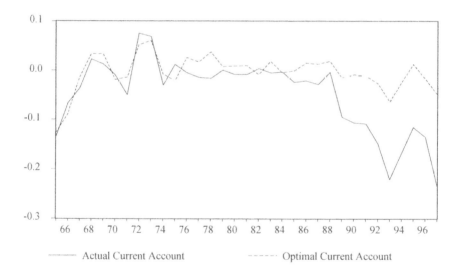

    ——— Actual Current Account   ----- Optimal Current Account

Figure 8.3   Actual and Optimal Current Account

Asymmetrical access to the international financial market on the optimal current account modifies, as discussed earlier in Chapter 4, the testable PVMCA equation to:

$$hz_t = -\sum_{t=T+1}^{\infty} \beta^{t-T}(g_1 - g_2)^{t-T} z_t \qquad (8.6)$$

where, as discussed in section 4.5 of Chapter 4, $z_t = (\Delta Q^h_t, \Delta Q^l_t, CA^h_t, CA^l_t, \hat{r})'$, $g_1 = [1\ 1\ 0\ 0\ 0]$, $g_2 = [0\ 0\ 0\ 0\ 1]$, $h = [0\ 0\ 1\ 1\ 0]$. ΔQ^h_t (ΔQ^l_t) equals ΔQ_t when it is positive (negative) but is zero when it is negative or equal to zero (positive or equal to zero). Similarly, CA^h_t (CA^l_t) equals CA_t when it is positive (negative) but is zero when it is negative or equal to zero (positive or equal to zero). $\hat{r}$ is the consumption-based interest rate incorporating the world real interest rate and expected changes in the exchange rate. Rewrite equation (8.6) as:

$$CA_t^{**} = k\ z_t \qquad (8.7)$$

where $k = -(g_1 - g_2)\beta\psi\ (I - \beta\psi)^{-1}$.

A test of asymmetry inn access to the financial market entails the estimation of the k vector and its comparison with the expected theoretical value of [0 0 1 1 0]. The estimated value of the k vector is [0.02 -0.05 0.78 1.15 0.08], which is not quite different from the expected theoretical value. The χ^2 of the Wald test of the parameter restrictions is 5.82 and its p-value of 0.11 implies a weak acceptance of the PVMCA extended to incorporate asymmetric access to the international financial market. The acceptance of the extended model suggests that the capital controls associated with the control regimes and the political and macroeconomic sources of instability in the Ghanaian economy prevented private economic agents from using the international financial market to smooth consumption. However, the volatility of the predicted current account is 30 percent higher than of the actual current account. This also validates the imposition on the model of asymmetric access to international financial markets: the current account could not be used to smooth consumption when there is limited access to the international capital markets. Figure 8.4 below graphs the actual current account and the optimal one under asymmetric access to international financial markets. The predicted current account is relatively close to the actual current account during both the pre-ERP period and the post-ERP period.

According to the intertemporal models of the current account, an expected rise in future income over that of current income leads to an increase in current consumption and a reduction in saving, so that if investment does not change, the current account must deteriorate. With asymmetric access to the international market, the relationship between the expected rise in output and the deterioration in the current account weakens. Conversely, if private agents expect a decline in future income from that in the current period, they will reduce current consumption, so that, with present income unchanged, saving will increase. If investment remains constant, domestic agents will lend part of this saving abroad, which will improve the current account. If the assumption of asymmetric access is binding, then CA^h_t will Granger-cause ΔQ^j_t, but CA^j_t will not Granger-cause ΔQ^h_t. To test for this effect, we estimated a one lag, five-variable VAR including ΔQ^h_t, ΔQ^j_t, CA^h_t, CA^j_t, and $\hat{r}$ variables. Our estimations show that the null hypothesis of no Granger-causality between CA^h_t and ΔQ^j_t is rejected at the 5 percent significance level. The F-statistic is 4.30 and the p-value is 0.02. Further, the null hypothesis of no Granger-causality between CA^j_t and ΔQ^h_t is not rejected at the 5 percent significance level with an F-statistic of 0.81 and a p-value of 0.45. Once again these results confirm the existence of asymmetric access in international financial markets.

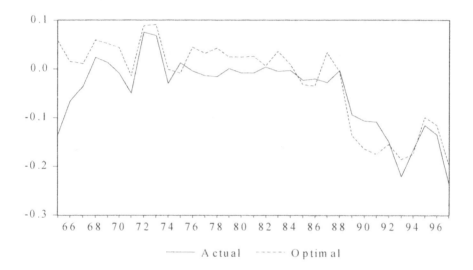

Figure 8.4   Actual and Optimal Current Account

Conclusions

The purpose of this chapter has been to conduct an econometric analysis of Ghana's current account based on the present value model of the current account (PVMCA) over the period from 1960 to 2000. The use of this model is based on its ability to obtain an optimal current account series which is consistent with the joint hypothesis of consumption smoothing behaviour on the part of economic agents and intertemporal solvency. The optimal current account series can be compared with the actual current account series and used to judge the excessiveness of the actual current account series. In comparison with most empirical studies that apply the PVMCA to developing economies, this book extended the benchmark present value model of the current account to include changes in the interest rate, the exchange rate, the terms of trade and asymmetry in access to the international financial market.

The econometric analysis conducted in this chapter has shown that the present value approach to modelling the current account is capable of explaining the dynamics of the actual current account provided that changes in the interest rate and the exchange rate are incorporated into the model. The benchmark PVMCA failed to explain satisfactorily the cyclical movements in Ghana's current account. This failure can be ascribed to the reason that in the case of a developing country that relies heavily on exports of a few goods and external funds for development efforts, changes in the interest rate and exchange rates are important determinants of the current account balances. This was confirmed by our results for the extended model. The extended model explains the dynamics in the actual current account data and the full magnitude of the fluctuations. Our results imply that changes in the international interest rates and exchange rates, business investment decisions and government policies, as well as the consumption-smoothing behaviour of private agents, impact on the Ghanaian current account.

Finally, the hypothesis of asymmetry in access to the international financial market was not rejected, confirming that agents in Ghana do have restricted access to the international financial markets. Due to macroeconomic and political instability in Ghana, growth potential is reduced and economic agents' ability to pay back borrowed funds is reduced. International financial market perceiving this may not lend to economic agents in Ghana to smooth consumption when there is a negative shock. However, economic agents in Ghana can easily lend abroad whenever there is a positive shock.

Data Appendix 8.I

	Per capita Real GDP (Cedis)	Per capita private cons. (Cedis)	Per Capita Invest. (Cedis)	Per Capita Govt. Expend. (Cedis)	World Int. Rate	Real Effective Exch. Rate	Terms of Trade
1960	481426	383593	226618	53061	na	68.14	100.5
1961	495216	427203	213070	58448	na	53.07	109.9
1962	503141	418864	180162	61567	na	54.85	124.0
1963	505212	420322	196853	63323	0.93	45.05	170.4
1964	502081	400609	194013	64941	1.72	37.35	169.8
1965	496630	383821	179207	71818	1.85	30.63	124.6
1966	486753	385105	126017	63489	2.25	28.02	136.2
1967	463583	359092	101408	69352	2.24	42.81	153.7
1968	484800	341641	107226	81275	2.27	41.23	211.3
1969	503562	367532	108571	71793	7.65	40.62	210.5
1970	525762	387281	137550	67494	3.64	41.98	269.4
1971	540671	414420	143544	70042	1.68	77.87	116.3
1972	512031	381249	80760	64572	0.81	51.71	148.8
1973	572596	428221	95160	62459	2.01	45.08	165.1
1974	575404	443036	14360	70258	-1.52	44.65	144.5
1975	488847	358376	119088	63754	-2.66	36.32	119.4
1976	461597	365755	86293	56514	-2.05	24.83	166.4
1977	463180	358412	94768	58462	-2.14	13.62	232.7
1978	493125	410577	65230	55713	1.97	22.10	203.2
1979	467181	388269	61977	48055	3.39	15.92	194.5
1980	454755	381532	53304	50767	2.87	11.79	192.0
1981	432343	377542	40244	38056	7.01	5.15	175.0
1982	386833	347313	26731	25071	6.35	4.12	119.0
1983	374882	340476	28157	21972	4.63	19.25	162.0
1984	370623	319202	50887	26904	6.21	21.21	125.0
1985	376170	312102	71842	35353	4.14	28.38	114.0
1986	383334	311406	71521	42425	3.78	39.07	128.0
1987	390067	319160	81112	39054	3.84	66.93	124.0
1988	400608	317950	87288	39945	4.41	64.70	118.0
1989	409507	342912	110639	42029	4.69	68.65	100.0
1990	411457	351590	100592	44955	3.21	67.13	94.0
1991	421242	349157	113547	51048	1.63	67.18	96.0
1992	425461	354952	58609	60729	0.35	77.19	90.0
1993	434230	341855	103306	63713	0.22	97.93	83.0
1994	436586	321652	98511	59911	2.30	110.55	90.0
1995	442760	337521	93548	53450	3.20	100.00	100.0
1996	452133	344068	92985	54451	2.91	82.46	99.0
1997	460395	367542	108895	56884	5.86	79.28	100.0

Source: IMF: International Financial Statistics.

Chapter 9

Summary and Conclusions

Given that the focus of this book is on West Africa, Nigeria and Ghana were chosen for our comparative analysis because they constitute the two largest English-speaking economies in the West African region. The evolution of these economies in terms of macroeconomic variables, their structural changes and exposure to external shocks make an explanation of their current account a useful exercise both from their own perspective, the perspective of other African economies, as well as of developing ones generally.

The theories for the determination of the current account of the balance of payments can be classified into two broad categories. One of these consists of the traditional approaches consisting of the elasticities approach, the absorption approach and the monetary approach, where the last one really deals with the balance of payments as a whole. These are essentially one-period or timeless analyses. The second category consists of intertemporal approaches, which focus on multiple periods, especially the lifetime of the consumer at the level of the individual. The dominant approach in this category is the present value, intertemporal, approach to the current account (PVMCA). The basic model of this approach at the individual's level determines his optimal consumption and saving over his lifetime, as in the Life-Cycle Consumption Hypothesis, as a function of his income. Under the assumption that the consumer wants to have an even consumption path, he will save in periods when his income exceeds the average amount of the present discounted value of his lifetime incomes. Since this saving is in real (commodity) terms, it would be as if he sold the excess commodities from his production to others. Conversely, when his income is less than the average amount of the present discounted value of his lifetime incomes, he will dissave. Since this dissaving is in real (commodity) terms, it would be as if he bought the excess commodities from his production to others. In the aggregate over all consumers and in open economies without any hindrances to trade, this behaviour translates to the private saving being either used for public dissaving (i.e., fiscal deficits), investment or net export. That is, the net exports of a country will equal its output less its private consumption, government deficits and domestic investment. Defining the sum of the latter items as total domestic consumption (really, usage) of commodities and output less this domestic consumption as 'net output' (not used in the domestic economy, thereby becoming available for export), net exports will equal this net output. If average expected net output over the future is expected to rise above the current one, total domestic consumption will exceed net output in the current period, the excess consumption will be financed by positive net imports (negative net exports) of commodities. Conversely, if average expected net output over the future is expected to rise above the current one, total domestic consumption will exceed net output in the current period, the excess consumption will be financed by positive net imports (negative net exports) of commodities. This procedure derives the optimal value of net exports from an intertemporal model of consumption such as the Life-Cycle Consumption Hypothesis, and is at the core of the PVMCA.

Since net exports generate an inflow of foreign exchange for the economy and net imports generate an outflow of foreign exchange for the economy, balance of payments equilibrium requires offsetting capital flows. The benchmark/benchmark PVMCA assumes perfect capital mobility, so that net imports are financed by a corresponding capital inflow while net exports lead to a matching capital outflow. This benchmark PVMCA has a number of inherent weaknesses, which include its exclusion of changes in the interest rate, exchange rate and terms of trade. It also fails to allow for the fact that agents may not have unrestricted access to the international financial market in the face of, for example, an unexpected deterioration in the terms of trade.

Capital flows depend on interest rate differentials and movements in the exchange rate, so that we need an extension of the PVMCA to incorporate their impact into the determination of net exports. This book's theoretical development of this version of the PVMCA combines changes in the interest rate, exchange rates and terms of trade in order to derive the consumption-based interest rate. Further, other developing countries, just as Nigeria and Ghana do, may face the prospect that it is easier for them to export capital but more difficult – because of regulations or imperfections in the international capital markets – to import it. This implies an asymmetry in access to foreign capital markets. Therefore, the possibility of asymmetry in capital flows needs to be taken into account. Doing so provides another extension of the PVMCA.

This book investigates the appropriateness of using various versions of the PVMCA for analysing the current account balances of Nigeria and Ghana. It starts with the theoretical specification of the benchmark version of PVMCA, which assumes constant interest rates, exchange rates and terms of trade. This version also assumes perfect access to international financial markets. The book then explores the applications of extended versions of the PVMCA to the current accounts of Nigeria and Ghana by introducing changes in the interest rate, exchange rate, terms of trade and asymmetry in access to the international financial market.

Given the reoccurring and persistent current account deficits in both Nigeria and Ghana during the periods covered by this book, the analysis was further extended to examine the issue of excessiveness and sustainability of current account deficits. This is also a useful exercise from the perspective of developing countries generally since they often face similar persistent current account deficits.

In terms of the sequence of the theoretical analysis presented, the book first presents the general theoretical framework and justification for the analysis of the current account balance in an intertemporal context. This results in the benchmark PVMCA, which excludes changes in the interest rate, exchange rate and terms of trade. The theoretical extension of this benchmark PVMCA to accommodate changes in the interest rate, the exchange rate, and the terms of trade was then derived. The resulting model was further extended to accommodate possible asymmetry in access to the international financial market.

This book tested the several versions of the PVMCA models on data on the Nigerian and Ghanaian economies. Our empirical estimations of the different versions of the PVMCA for these economies showed that the appropriate current account model must accommodate the channels through which changes in the external shocks impact on the current account. The channel through which external shocks impact on the current account proved to be significant. The book also did not reject the hypothesis of asymmetry in access to the international financial markets in the context of both economies.

For purposes of comparison with the PVMCA, this book also examined the traditional approaches (elasticities, absorption and monetary ones) to modelling the current account. Each of these traditional approaches lacks intertemporal underpinnings. The econometric specification of the determinants of the current account based on these traditional models and other variables were investigated. The PVMCA and the traditional (elasticities, absorption and monetary) models of the current account were compared for Nigeria. Our conclusion from this comparison is that the PVMCA outperforms the traditional approaches. In addition, on purely theoretical grounds, since economic agents and the economy do not function for only one period or in a timeless context, and since economic agents make decisions in the present in the light of their information on their future incomes, etc., the intertemporal underpinnings of the PVMCA make it preferable to the traditional approaches.

For most of the periods covered in this book, the current account balances of both Nigeria and Ghana were in deficit. The PVMCA provides an estimate of the optimal current account balance that can be met by future periods. This estimate was compared with the actual current balance in order to determine whether the current account deficits were excessive relative to the optimal ones, and, therefore, relative to the economy's future net output. A finding of excessive deficits is indicative of potential future problems in meeting the required payments to foreigners.

For Nigeria, given its historical experience of recurring current account deficits and increases in the external debt to GDP ratio in most years, the sustainability of the current account imbalances was examined by determining the excessiveness of the current account imbalances.

Our empirical finding is that the appropriate version of the present value approach to the current account is a valid theoretical framework for the determination of the current account balances for both Nigeria and Ghana. This appropriate version of current account determination needs to incorporate the channels through which external shocks impact upon the current account. They must also consider intratemporal and intertemporal effects that are associated with external shocks, such as to the terms of trade. In terms of the implications for policy, our finding is that policy makers need knowledge of the private sector responses to external shocks in formulating their policies for dealing with internal and external shocks.

On the question of the excessiveness of current account balances relative to the optimal ones implied by the PVMCA for both unconstrained and constrained access to foreign financial markets, we found that the Nigerian current account deficits were excessive in the period preceding the external crisis of 1986. This was especially so during 1981-83. The strict trade and exchange policy measures adopted during 1984-85 curbed this trend. However, the unsustainability of such policy measures was reflected in a dramatic re-emergence and widening of the gap between the actual and optimal current account balance in 1986. Further, for most of the years, Nigeria's optimal current account deficit, in the absence of unrestricted access to the international financial market, was greater than the optimal current account that allows for possible asymmetry of capital flows. We conclude that improvements in the access to the international financial markets, and ensuring symmetry between capital outflows and inflows, would have improved the current account balance position.

For Nigeria, the current account balances were also compared with the benchmark ones derived from maintaining the ratio of external debt-to-GDP ratio constant over time. Another method for judging the sustainability of current account deficits is to use the relevant macroeconomic and structural indicators to determine their sustainable levels. A finding of significant levels of unsustainable current account deficits can be taken as indicative of the potential for the occurrence of external crisis. For Nigeria, our use of a wide array of macroeconomic and structural factors to assess the sustainability of the Nigerian current account deficits in the period preceding the 1986 external crisis revealed their unsustainability.

Our conclusion from this examination of sustainability is that current account deficits associated with exchange rate appreciation and fiscal deficits appear not to be sustainable. Current account deficits that are associated with low savings, high concentration of exports in a particular commodity, lower economic growth, growing external debt, and high debt servicing, inadequate foreign exchange reserves and political instability, could easily degenerate into an external crisis. Therefore, countries should have a floating exchange rate and pursue low fiscal deficits or a balanced budget. They should also promote increased saving rates, diversification of the export base and higher growth rates, as well as pursuing efficient debt-management strategies.

While our empirical analyses for Ghana are not as extensive as those for Nigeria, our tests of the various versions of the PVMCA for Ghana provide information on its current account determination and, in addition, permit a check on the results derived on Nigeria. In addition, the comparisons allow a better basis for the assessment on the application of the PVMCA approach generally to developing and small, open economies.

Our overall review of the Ghanaian economy had as its focus the association between the evolution of its macroeconomic policies and internal and external balances. This included a review of the different trade and payments regimes followed and their impact on the external sector of the Ghanaian economy. During the period studied, the Ghanaian economic policies changed from an inward-looking strategy to a more liberal economic regime, with a quite different impact on Ghana's growth performance, inflation and external balances. The recurring pattern that emerged was that anytime there was a change in the trade regime and macroeconomic stance, the performance of the external economy was affected very significantly. In addition, the performance of the external sector of the Ghanaian economy differed significantly between the pre-Economic Recovery Program (ERP) era (which was associated with various levels of control regimes) and the post-ERP era. Whereas the trade and payment controls in the pre-ERP era were able to ensure some current account surpluses, the increasingly liberal trade and payment regimes that were followed during the post-ERP registered current account deficits.

Our findings from the application of the different versions of the PVMCA to the Ghanaian economy were similar to those for Nigeria. While the benchmark PVMCA was rejected for the Ghanaian economy, this was not so for the extended PVMCA incorporating changes in interest and exchange rates. However, the introduction of the terms of trade to the model did not improve its performance for Ghana's current account. As for Nigeria, the assumption of asymmetry in access to the international financial market was not rejected for Ghana. This finding implies some degree of restricted access to the international financial markets. The implication of this result is simple. If the international financial markets perceive that there is a risk associated with lending to economic agents in Ghana due to political and economic instability, capital inflows to fund desired levels of domestic consumption and current account deficits would be inadequate. In this case, economic agents would not be able to achieve adequate consumption smoothing when current output falls below the expected average future one.

Both Nigeria and Ghana have very similar economic and political stages and are at a somewhat similar stage of economic development, though differing in that Nigeria is an oil exporter and Ghana is an oil importer. Given their similarities, they provide similar conclusions on the determination of their current accounts. Further, our study of their macroeconomic indicators also points to very similar policy recommendations of the appropriateness of floating exchange rates and prudent fiscal policies.

In terms of contributions to studies on the Nigerian and Ghanaian economies, this book is the first attempt at estimating for them a PVMCA that includes changes in interest and rates and in terms of trade. This book is also, to our knowledge, the first one to perform analysis of the sustainability and excessiveness of current account deficits for any sub-Saharan African country. In terms of the theoretical contributions for the study of developing economies generally, this book represents the first attempt at modifying the benchmark PVMCA to incorporate the terms of trade and possible asymmetry in access to the international financial market.

References

Adedeji, O. S. (2001a), 'Consumption-Based Interest Rate and the Present-Value Model of the Current Account – Evidence from Nigeria'. *IMF* Working Paper no. 93.

Adedeji, O. S. (2001b), 'The Excessiveness and Sustainability of the Nigerian Current Account'. *IMF* Working Paper no. 87.

Adedeji, O. S. (2002), *The Intertemporal Approach to Modeling the Current Account: Evidence from Nigeria*. Doctoral dissertation, McGill University.

Adedeji, O. S. and Handa, J. (2005a), 'The Present Value Model of the Current Account for Developing Economies: The evidence from Nigeria', Unpublished paper.

Adedeji, O. S. and Handa, J. (2005b), 'The Size and Sustainability of the Nigerian Current Account Deficits', Unpublished paper.

Ahmed, S. (1986), 'Temporary and Permanent Government Spending in an Open Economy', *Journal of Monetary Economics* 17, pp. 197-224.

Ajayi, S. I. (1995), 'Capital Flight and External Debt in Nigeria', *Research Paper* No. 35. Nairobi: African Economic Research Consortium.

Alexander, S. (1952), 'Effects of Devaluation on the Trade Balance', *IMF Staff Papers* 2, pp. 263-78.

Bergin, P. R. and Sheffrin, S. M. (2000), 'Interest Rates, Exchange Rates and Present Value Models of the Current Account', *The Economic Journal* 110, pp. 535-58.

Bhagwati, J. D. (1978), *Foreign Trade Regimes and Economic Development, pp. Anatomy and Consequences of Exchange Controls*. New York: Ballinger for the National Bureau of Economic Research.

Blanchard, O. J. (1983), 'Debt and the Current Account Deficits in Brazil', in *Financial Policies and the World Capital Market: The Problem of Latin American Countries*, Pedro, A. A. Dornbusch, R. and Obstfeld, M., eds. Chicago: University of Chicago Press.

Buiter, W. H. (1981), 'Time Preference and International Lending and Borrowing in an Overlapping-Generations Model', *Journal of Political Economy* 89, pp. 769-97.

Callen, T. and Cashin, P. (1999), 'Assessing External Sustainability in India', *IMF Working Paper* No. 181.

Campbell, J. Y. (1987), 'Does Saving Anticipate Declining Labor Income? An Alternative Test of the Permanent Income Hypothesis', *Econometrica* 55, pp. 1249-74.

Campbell, J. Y. and Mankiw, N. G. (1989), 'Consumption, Income, and Interest Rates: Reinterpreting the Time Series Evidence', *NBER Macroeconomics Annual*. Cambridge: MA, MIT Press, pp. 185-215.

Campbell, J. and Shiller, R. (1987), 'Cointegration and Test of Present Value Models', *Journal of Political Economy* 95, pp. 1062-88.

Campbell, J. Y. Lo, A. W. and Mackinlay, A. C. (1997), *The Econometrics of Financial Markets*. Princeton: Princeton University Press.

Cardia, E. (1997), 'Replacing Ricardian Equivalence Tests with Simulated Series', *The American Economic Review* 87, pp. 65-79.

Carroll, C. and Samwick, A. (1995), 'The Nature of Precautionary Wealth', *Working Paper* No. 5193. Cambridge, MA, National Bureau of Economic Research.

Cashin, P. and McDermott J. (1996), 'Are Australia's Current Account Deficits Excessive?' *IMF Working Paper* No. 85.

Central Bank of Nigeria (1998), *Statistical Bulletin*. Abuja: Central Bank of Nigeria.

Cooper, R. and Sachs, J. (1985), 'Borrowing Abroad: The Debtor's Perspective,' In *International Debt and Developing Countries*, Cuddington, T. J. and Smith, G. W, eds. World Bank.

Corsetti, G. Pesenti, P. and Roubini, N. (1998), 'What Caused the Asian Currency and Financial Crisis? Part I: A Macroeconomic Overview'. *Working Papers* No. 6833. Cambridge: MA, National Bureau of Economic Research.

Cuddington, J. T. (1986), 'Capital Flight: Estimates, Issues and Explanations', *Studies in International Finance* 58. New Jersey: Department of Economics, Princeton University.

Darku, A. and Handa, J. (2005), 'Empirical Analysis of the Current Account of Ghana in the context of Rational Intertemporal Decisions', Unpublished paper.

Deaton, A. (1989), 'Savings in Developing Countries', in *Proceedings of the World Bank Conference on Development Economics*, Stanley F. and de Tray, D. eds. Washington, DC: The World Bank, pp. 61-108.

Dolado, J., Jenkinson, T. and Simon, SR. (1990), 'Cointegration and Unit Roots', *Journal of Economic Surveys* 3, pp. 249-273.

Dornbusch, R. (1983), 'Real Interest Rates, Home Goods and Optimal External Borrowing', *Journal of Political Economy* 91, pp. 141-153.

Edwards, S. (1989), *Real Exchange Rates, Devaluation, and Adjustment: Exchange Rate Policy in Developing Countries*. Cambridge: MA, MIT Press.

Edwards, S. and Montiel, P. J. (1989), 'Devaluation Crises and the Macroeconomic Consequences of Postponed Adjustment in Developing countries', *IMF Staff Papers* 36, pp. 875-903.

Edwards, S. and Santaella, J. A. (1993), 'Devaluation Controversies in Developing countries: Lessons from the Bretton Woods Era', in *A Retrospective on the Bretton Woods System: Lessons for International Monetary Reform*. Bordo, M.D. and Eichengreen, B. eds. Chicago: University of Chicago Press, pp. 405-55.

Egwaikhide, F. O. (1997), 'Effects of Budget Deficits on the Current Account Balance in Nigeria: A Simulation Exercise', *Research Paper* No.70. Nairobi: African Economic Research Consortium.

Elbadawi, I. A. and Soto, R. (1995). 'Real Exchange Rates and Macroeconomic Adjustment in Sub-Saharan Africa and Other Developing Countries'. Paper presented for the Bi-Annual Research Workshop of the African Economic Research Consortium, Johannesburg.

Engle, R.F. (1982), 'Autoregressive Conditional Heteroscedasticity with Estimates of the Variances of U. K. Inflation', *Econometrica* 50, pp. 987-1008.

Enunenwosu, C. E. (1984), 'Balance of Payments in Nigeria, 1970-80', In *Trade and Development in Economic Community of West African States* (ECOWAS), Orimalade, A., and Ubogu, R. E., eds. New Delhi: Vikas Publishing House.

Fakiyesi, T. and Umo, J. U. (1995), 'Profiles and Determinants of Nigeria's Balance of Payments: The Current Account Component, 1950-88', *Research Paper* No. 45. Nairobi: African Economic Research Consortium.

Frankel, J. and Johnson, H. G. (1976), *The Monetary Approach to the Balance of Payments*. London: Allen & Unwin.

Frankel, J. and Rose, A. K. (1996), 'Currency Crashes in Emerging Markets: An Empirical Treatment', *Journal of International Economics* 41, pp. 351-66.

Gersovitz, M. (1988), 'Saving and Development,' In *Handbook of Development Economics*, Chenery, H. B and Srinivasan, T. N., eds. Amsterdam: North Holland.

Ghartey, E. (1987), Devaluation as a Balance of Payments Correction Measure in Developing Countries: A Study relating to Ghana', *Applied Economics* 19, pp. 937-47.

Ghosh, A. R. (1995), 'International Capital Mobility Among the Major Industrialized Countries: Too Little or too Much?' *Economic Journal* 105, pp. 107-28.

Ghosh, A. R. and Ostry, J. D. (1995), 'The Current Account in Developing Countries: A Perspective from The Consumption-Smoothing Approach', *The World Bank Economic Review* 9, pp 305-33.

Granger, C. W. J. (1969), 'Investigating Causal Relations by Econometric Models and Cross-Spectral Methods', *Econometrica* 37, pp. 424-38.

Grimard, F. (1997), 'Household Consumption Smoothing through Ethnic Ties: Evidence from Côte d'Ivoire', *Journal of Development Economics* 53, pp. 391-422.

Hall, R. E. (1978), 'Stochastic Implications of the Life-Cycle Permanent Income Hypothesis: Theory and Evidence', *Journal of Political Economy* 86, pp. 971-87.

Handa, J. (2000), *Monetary Economics*. New York: Routledge.

Harrigan, J. and Oduro, A. D. (1997), 'Exchange Rate Policies and the Balance of Payments in Ghana: 1972-1996', *Discussion Paper Series* No. 9725. The University of Manchester, School of Economic Studies.

Hayashi, F. (1982), 'The Permanent Income Hypothesis: Estimation and Testing by Instrumental Variables', *Journal of Political Economy* 90, pp. 895-916.

Hercowitz, Z. (1986), 'On the Determination of the External Debt: The Case of Israel', *Journal of International Money and Finance* 5, pp. 315-34.

Hooper, P. and Marquez, J. (1995), 'Exchange Rate, Prices and External Adjustment in the United States and Japan', in *Understanding Interdependence: The Macroeconomics of the Open Economy*, Kenen, P., ed. Princeton, NJ, Princeton University Press.

Huang, C., and Lin, K. S. (1993), 'Deficits, Government Expenditures, and Tax Smoothing in the United States: 1929-1988', *Journal of Monetary Economics* 31, pp. 317-39.

IMF (1977), *The Monetary Approach to the Balance of Payments*. Washington, DC: IMF.

Islam, R. and Wetzel, D. (1994), 'Ghana: Adjustment, Reform and Growth', in Easterly, W., Rodriguez, C., and Shmidt-Hebbel, K., eds. *Public Sector Deficits and Macroeconomic Performance*. World Bank: Washington, DC.

Jebuni, C. D. Oduro, A. D. and Tutu, K. A. (1994), 'Trade and Payments Regime and the Balance of Payments in Ghana', *World Development* 22, pp. 1161-173.

Johnson, D. (1986), 'Consumption, Permanent Income and Financial Wealth in Canada: Empirical Evidence on the Intertemporal Approach to the Current Account', *Canadian Journal of Economics* 29, pp.189-206.

Johnson, H. G. (1970) 'Fiscal Policy and the Balance of Payments', in Taylor, M. C., ed. *Taxation for African Economic Development*. London: Hutchinson Educational Ltd.

Kaminsky, G. Lizondo, S. and Reinhart, C. M. (1998), 'Leading Indicators of Currency Crises', *IMF Staff Papers* 45, pp. 1-45.

Khan, M. and Knight, M. (1983), 'Determinants of Current Account Balances of non-oil Developing Countries in the 1970s: An Empirical Analysis', *IMF Staff Papers* 30, pp. 97-107.

Komolafe, O. S. (1996), 'Exchange Rate Policy and Nigeria's External Sector Performance: Implications for the Future', *The Nigerian Journal of Economic and Social Studies* 38, pp. 65-90.

Kravis, I. Heston, A. and Summers, R. (1982), *World Product and Income: International Comparisons and Real GDP*. Baltimore: MD, Johns Hopkins University Press.

Krueger, A. (1986), 'Problems of Liberalization,' in Choksi, A. and Papageorgiou, D., eds. *Economic Liberalization in Developing Countries*. Oxford: Blackwell.

Krugman, P. R. (1979), 'A Model of Balance of Payments Crises', *Journal of Money, Credit, and Banking* 11, pp. 311-25.

Lucas, R. E. Jr. (1976), 'Econometric Policy Evaluation: A Critique', *Carnegie-Rochester Conference Series on Public Policy* 1, pp. 19-46.

Makrydakis, S. (1999), 'Consumption-Smoothing and the Excessiveness of Greece's Current Account Deficits', *Empirical Economics* 24, pp. 183-209.

Mascollel, A., Whinston, M. and Green, J. (1995), *Microeconomic Theory*. Oxford: Oxford University Press.

McGettigan, D. (1999), 'Current Account and External Sustainability in the Baltics, Russia, and Other Countries of the Former Soviet Union', *Occasional Paper* No. 189. Washington: IMF.

Meade, J. E. (1951), *The Balance of Payments*. Oxford: Oxford University Press.

Milbourne, R. and Otto, G. (1992), 'Consumption Smoothing and the Current Account', *Australian Economic Papers* No. 59, pp. 369-84.

Milesi-Ferretti, G. M. and Razin, A. (1996), 'Current-Account Sustainability'. *Princeton Studies in International Finance* No. 81. Princeton, NJ: Princeton University Press.

Mwau, G. and Handa, J. (1995), *Rational Economic Decisions and Current Account in Kenya*. Aldershot: Averbury Ashgate Publishing.

Nyatepe-Coo, A. A. (1993), 'External Disturbances, Domestic Policy Responses and Debt Accumulation in Nigeria', *World Development* 21, pp. 1621-31.

Obstfeld, M. (1982), 'Aggregate Spending and the Terms of Trade: Is there a Laursen-Metzler Effect?' *Quarterly Journal of Economics* 97, pp. 251-70.

Obstfeld, M. (1986), 'Capital Mobility in the World Economy: Theory and Measurement', *Carnegie-Rochester Conference Series on Public Policy* 24, pp. 55-103.

Obstfeld, M. and Rogoff, K. (1996), *Foundations of International Macroeconomics*. Cambridge, MA: The MIT Press.

Ojo, O. (1973), 'A Medium-Term Planning Model of the Nigerian Economy', *The Nigerian Journal of Economic and Social Studies* 15, pp. 125-50.

Olayide, S. O. (1968), 'Import Demand Model: An Econometric Analysis of Nigeria's Import Trade', *The Nigerian Journal of Economic and Social Studies* 10, pp. 303-20.

Osagie, E. (1973), 'Balance of Payments in Nigeria: A Methodological Note on Concepts and Measurement', *The Nigerian Journal of Economic and Social Studies*, pp. 39-52.

Oshikoya, W. T. (1990), 'Balance of Payments Experience of Nigeria: 1960-86.' *Journal of Developing Areas* 25, pp. 69-92.

Ostry, J. D. (1988), 'Balance of Trade, Terms of Trade, and Real Exchange Rate: An Intertemporal Optimizing Framework', *IMF Staff Papers* 35, pp. 541-73.

Ostry, J. D. and Reinhart. C. M. (1992), 'Private Savings and Terms of Trade Shocks: Evidence from Developing Countries', *IMF Staff Papers* 39, pp. 495-517.

Otto, G. (1992), 'Testing a Present Value Model of the Current Account: Evidence from U.S. and Canadian Time series', *Journal of International Money and Finance* 11, pp. 414-30.

Pastor, M. (1989), 'Current Account Deficits and Debt Accumulation in Latin America: Debate and Evidence', *Journal of Development Economics* 31, pp. 77-97.

Persson, T. and Svensson, L. E. (1985), 'Current Account Dynamics and the Terms of Trade: Harberger-Laursen-Metzler Two Generations Later', *Journal of Political Economy* 93, pp. 43-65.

Phillips, P. C. B. and Perron, P. (1988), 'Testing for a Unit Root in Time Series Regression', *Biometrika* 75, pp. 165-93.

Polak, J. J. (1957), 'Monetary Analysis of Income Formation and Payments Problems', *IMF Staff Papers* 6, pp. 1-50.

Polak, J. J. (2001). 'The Two Monetary Approaches to the Balance of Payments: Keynesian and Johnsonian', *IMF Working Paper* 100.

Roubini, N. (1988), 'Current Account and Budget Deficits in an Intertemporal Model of Consumption and Taxation Smoothing: A Solution to the Feldstein-Horioka Puzzle?' Working Paper No. 2773. Cambridge: MA, National Bureau of Economic Research.

Sachs, J. (1982), 'The Current Account in the Macroeconomic Adjustment Process', *Scandinavian Journal of Economics* 84, pp. 147-59.

Said, S.E. and Dickey, D. A. (1984), 'Testing for Unit Roots in Autoregressive Moving Average Models of Unknown Order', *Biometrica* 71, pp. 599-607.

Sheffrin, S. and Woo, W. T. (1990), 'Present Value Tests of an Intertemporal Model of the Current Account', *Journal of International Economics* 29, pp. 237-53.

Stockman, A. C. and Svensson, L. E. (1987), 'Capital Flows, Investment, and Exchange Rates', *Journal of Monetary Economics* 19, pp. 171-201.

Svensson, L. E. O. and Razin, A. (1983), 'The Terms of Trade and the Current Account: The Harberger-Laursen Metzler Effect', *Journal of Political Economy* 91, pp. 97-125.

World Bank, (1985), *World Development Report*. Washington, DC: World Bank.

Index